AND PILATE SAID——

AT THE "POOLS OF SOLOMON"

A vital link in the investigation described in this book. Specially reproduced from a negative taken prior to the modern restoration of the reservoirs

AND PILATE SAID—

A New Study of the Roman Procurator

by

FRANK MORISON (pseud.)

Ross, Albert Henry

NEW YORK
CHARLES SCRIBNER'S SONS
1940

To my Friends

MR. and MRS. G. ERIC MATSON

to whom I am indebted for many unique
photographs specially taken for this book
and through whose unfailing courtesy and
kindness this Judean interlude will always
remain a fresh and inspiring memory

CONTENTS

7

LIST OF ILLUSTRATIONS

LIST OF ILLUSTRATIONS

LIST OF ILLUSTRATIONS

DIAGRAMS AND PLANS IN TEXT

CHAPTER I

DROPPING INTO LYDDA

HE would be a very unimaginative man who could drop suddenly one morning out of the skies into the little airport at Lydda—close to the immemorial foothills of the Judean range—and not be acutely conscious of the want of ceremony, the almost brutal informality of his approach.

Such recently was my experience.

I had gone to Palestine for a specific purpose and since this book is, in a sense, a report of what happened I should perhaps explain to the reader just why that journey was planned. It will help to justify, and, I hope, to commend to him, the rather personal and retrospective character of the narrative which follows.

Briefly, the circumstances were these:

About two years ago I was invited by the publishers of the present volume to write a biographical study of Pontius Pilate, a subject in which, for psychological and other reasons, I have always been deeply interested. A short sketch of the Roman Governor appeared in my book *Who Moved the Stone?* and it seemed to me that a fuller and more detailed account of the events of the Procuratorship was not only long overdue, but would be of interest to a wide circle of readers.

It so happened that I was busily engaged just then in seeing to press a work which had entailed nearly four years of arduous labour and I had little leisure for the extensive research which I knew this study would demand. I found time, however, to write to friends in Jerusalem for photographs and plans of certain ancient remains which throw light upon Pilate's activities during his period of office. I also took advantage of occasional opportunities to dip again into the numerous works on the archaeology of Palestine and the history of the first century which, under the pressure of other interests, had too long remained unopened in my library.

In due course the photographs arrived. The other book went to press and I was free at last to give undivided attention to the subject.

It quickly became evident, however, that there were literary and historical difficulties of no common order. In the first place very little of assured fact about Pontius Pilate is known. The relevant passages could almost be printed on a single sheet of paper and what the Gospels tell us concerning the actions of Pilate during the Great Tragedy have long been open to grave and bitter dispute. There are references, however, in the works of Philo of Alexandria and the historian Josephus which bear unmistakable evidence of resting upon fact and if these could be followed up and explored there might begin to

I. THE RUINED SITE OF ASCALON

"Tell it not in Gath; publish it not in the streets of Ascalon"

2. RAMLEH
A Picturesque View of the Tower of the Forty Martyrs

emerge the materials for a true historical estimate of the Procurator's character.

Unfortunately the difficulties were not confined to the relative paucity of the literary evidence. A great deal of Pilate's time was clearly devoted to an engineering enterprise which is not expressly referred to in the New Testament, but of which substantial remains exist to-day. I sought in vain for a full and detailed discussion of this important phase of the Procurator's activity. The recognized authorities upon the history of Judea in the first century were discreetly vague where this question was concerned and the archaeologists were usually so intent upon other and major problems that they frequently dismissed in a few inconclusive sentences matters which are obviously quite vital to our purpose.

After some fruitless efforts to obtain in London the specific information I required, I came to the conclusion that this study could only be pursued adequately in Jerusalem itself, where much specialized knowledge is concentrated and the visible remains are close at hand.

Despite, therefore, the stormy conditions then prevailing and the dangers attendant upon unescorted visits to the lonelier sorts of places in Palestine, I made plans to go to Jerusalem immediately the winter rains were over. In this way I felt I could best serve the interests of my prospective readers. The story should be written in the very shadow of those forbidding walls within which the most dramatic incidents in the life of Pilate and of his wife, Claudia, were enacted.

But there was, of course, something else—a very big Something!

Two destinies reached their supreme crisis on that dread morning in April, A.D. 29, when Pontius Pilate, by one solitary judicial act, changed the face of history.

I did not quite see how we could hope to give the Procurator a fair hearing—and I was determined that the hearing should be fair—without committing the reader in advance to certain far-reaching presuppositions concerning the character and motives of his Prisoner. The logical course was to trace the two histories to the point of intersection. But this involved a dual theme which might easily become unmanageable. It is against all the conventions to attempt the writing of two biographies under the cloak of one!

This problem was very much in my thoughts when I remembered something to which I drew attention in *Who Moved the Stone?*, viz. the very curious way in which the whole drama of the Passion pivoted upon certain explicit notices of *time*. The strength of the inferences which I then drew from these chronological coincidences has grown, rather than diminished, with the passage of the years and it seemed to me that if the reader could study what is reported in the Gospels, as it were at close quarters on the terrain itself, much that we are told about this unique event would become plain.

From that moment the plan of this book was clear.

Jerusalem first gave us the problem; she must now

help us to unravel it. We would go out to this ancient and tragic city—taking with us our archaeological difficulties and our historical uncertainties—and try to see the salient incidents of Pilate's career as though these memorable events had all happened yesterday, within our own personal and immediate experience. We should at least be the richer by a more intimate knowledge of the sites and we might encounter something which had previously escaped our notice.

With the registration of that decision I set about making plans for the journey.

CHAPTER II

A FIRST GLANCE AT THE PROBLEM

THREE things seemed to be necessary for the success of the project which I have briefly outlined in the preceding chapter.

First. That the time-table should be subordinated to the pursuit of certain specific investigations which I shall presently describe.

Second. That, wherever possible, the camera should be used to record the contemporary scene and those aspects of the terrain which can more effectively be portrayed visually.

Third. That we should make a conscious effort to rid our minds of all preconceptions and try to see the problem freshly —through critical modern eyes.

It was mainly for these reasons that I finally decided to go by air. A swift outward passage, *via* Rome and Alexandria, would bring us to Jerusalem within three days. My period of leave extended to one month and I felt that in that time, given fair weather, there would be a reasonable chance of completing the inquiries which I had in mind. The aerial approach, too, had this advantage: it gave a panoramic view of the road from

Egypt—one of the most ancient highways of the world—
and of certain unique features of the Judean landscape
to which the reader's attention will be drawn later.

Now it is a very sound rule of historical investigation
that, whenever possible, the present should be invoked
to illumine and interpret the past.

A man can doubtless obtain a good working idea of
the conditions of life, say, in a feudal castle of the thirteenth century, by travelling no farther than his own
library and confining his attention to a few well-chosen
books. But having laid that necessary foundation, let him
take a car and set out one morning across the Kentish
Weald. Let him climb the height of the downs about
Goudhurst and then drop down through many a leafy
lane to Bodiam. Here in a setting of superb English
beauty he will see the thing of which he has been reading,
a castle full-moated which in some magical way has
survived the ravages of time.

As though touched by an invisible wand, his imagination will spring suddenly to life. Here are the veritable
stones upon which the massive drawbridge once rested,
and across which mailed horsemen rode into the shelter
of this friendly fortress. Yonder is the level field, still
plainly marked out, where knightly jousts took place and
stirring feats of valour were performed. Beyond the dark
waters of the moat rise the battlemented towers, from
which men and women—very much like ourselves—must
often have peered anxiously in times of trouble or unrest
towards the distant fringe of trees, through which a

stealthy enemy might creep to within a bowshot of the castle.

In such a setting, and with this unique example before his eyes, the student will begin to understand some things which were, perhaps, only dimly perceived before. He will see, for example, why it was that a resourceful rebel, firmly entrenched in one of these castles, could dominate the countryside for a distance of many miles. Here, far from the central seat of Government was a reservoir of *armed* men, equipped with all the tools and resources for war or the chase. Here, too, were ample provisions for a siege. A determined posse of horsemen, sallying forth across the drawbridge, could swiftly impose its will upon any scattered communities within a day's ride from the castle. If danger threatened from superior forces, the defenders could ravage the countryside, withdraw behind the moat, and hold out almost interminably.

So it is with the study upon which we are now entering.

In the main we must rely for our facts about Pontius Pilate and his wife, Claudia, upon the recollections of two or three ancient writers who were almost contemporary with them. The importance of this written testimony is, of course, paramount and no later speculations, however stimulating to the imagination, must be allowed to compete with them. Side by side, however, with this contemporary witness lies something which the passage of twenty centuries has been unable to obliterate—the physical configuration of the land itself.

The modern traveller from Jericho to Jerusalem can

3. THE OLD JERICHO ROAD

Climbing to Jerusalem past the Inn of the Good Samaritan from the Wilderness of Judea

4. THE PLATFORM OF THE ROCK

Aerial photograph of the Temple Area, looking south, towards the village of Siloam

still climb laboriously up that winding and rocky ascent, past the Inn of the Good Samaritan, to Bethany and Bethphage. The city itself still stands upon those stony uplands, close to the ancient site of the Jebusite fortress which David stormed nearly three thousand years ago. From the summit of the Mount of Olives you can still look down upon the massive platform on which once stood the Temple of Herod, famed for its splendour and magnificence throughout the Graeco-Roman world. At the foot of the hill a greatly diminished Garden of Gethsemane, with its gnarled and ancient trees, passes at sunset, as of old, into the shadow of those forbidding walls.

All these things are part of the materials at our command, and we should, of course, be lacking in a sense of historical perspective if we failed to take advantage of them. Clearly, much more is needed, however, for an effective reconstruction of the events of those ten memorable years which Pontius Pilate spent in Judea, and I had in mind three main lines of investigation.

In the first place I very strongly desired to make a close personal inspection of the Roman remains at *Caesarea*, a place which in Pilate's time was a thriving centre of Oriental life, rivalling in importance, and in a sense overshadowing, Jerusalem itself. It was upon the busy quays of this ancient seaport that the Procurator first set foot when at the bidding of Tiberius he came to take up his new duties. It was here that he made his home, and at least one very significant incident of his career took place outside the white palace of Herod which looked down upon the tossing crowded waters of the harbour below.

Nearly sixty years have passed since Kitchener and Conder made their classic survey of the site, and I wanted, if possible, to wander unhindered among the sand dunes, to explore the great reef, to climb the rocky eminence upon which Strato's famous tower once stood, until imperceptibly there arose in imagination the outlines of the city which Pilate knew and whence a few years later St. Paul himself set sail upon one of the last and most perilous of his many voyages. I shall tell the story of that journey in a later chapter. It remains a haunting and very vivid memory.

My second line of inquiry proved to be of a much more difficult and complex character. It concerned the *water supply of Jerusalem* in ancient times and the steps taken by successive kings and rulers to safeguard and augment the rather scant resources which existed in the neighbourhood.

Josephus tells us that Pilate "brought water" to Jerusalem from a distance of two hundred stadia (approximately twenty-three miles) and, since the Procurator's activities in this connection caused one of the worst riots of his administration, resulting in much bloodshed and heavy loss of life, it became imperative to know just what purpose this undertaking was designed to serve and especially whether the destination of the water was the Temple itself.

The problem was complicated by the fact that there are well-preserved remains of *two* very ancient aqueducts originating in the neighbourhood of the so-called "Pools of Solomon" to the south-west of Jerusalem and archaeologists are by no means agreed as to the dating of these structures. There are also three subsidiary conduits which tradition ascribes to Herod the Great. The exploration of these channels from their sources near Hebron to the precincts of the city occupied a considerable amount of time.

In the end, however, this tracing of the aqueducts proved a study of absorbing interest, in which I was greatly helped by Mr. John D. Whiting, of the American Colony; by the Department of Antiquities in Jerusalem; by Dr. Sukenik, of the Hebrew University and by other specialist scholars resident in the district. I feel, therefore, that no apology will be needed for the comparatively large amount of space devoted to this deeply fascinating subject, since it throws light upon Pilate's motives in raiding the Sacred Treasury or Corban, an act for which he has, I think, been a little unfairly criticized.

Finally, I wished to make a series of rather peculiar *personal experiments and tests*, carried out in a reverent and inquiring spirit, upon the actual scene of the events so graphically described in the closing chapters of the four Gospels.

At first sight it may appear a matter of very small moment to inquire just how long it would take a man

23

engaged upon a desperate and urgent mission to pass from a certain point in the upper city to the site now occupied by the so-called Citadel of David. Or alternatively, what length of time would reasonably be occupied by a small group of persons proceeding without undue haste from the same point to the fork in the Bethany road at the foot of Olivet. Yet these and other vital determinations, which I made very carefully, watch in hand, have an important bearing upon the interpretation which we shall ultimately place upon the events.

Lest this should seem a strange and unfamiliar thought, the reader should bear in mind that there are two fundamentally divergent theories concerning the historical situation in Jerusalem on the eve of the fatal Passover. One is that presented to us in the quiet and restrained language of the Gospels, in which Jesus of Nazareth, of His own free will, and fully conscious of His unique destiny, submitted to, and even challenged, His own arrest. On this view Pontius Pilate, following the normal custom of the Procurators, was resident in Jerusalem throughout the whole period of the Feast.

The alternative is of a far more dramatic and revolutionary character. It presupposes a state of chaos and disorder in the Jewish capital, on the very eve of the Feast, which finds no parallel whatever in the New Testament.

According to this theory, which has been developed in great detail by Dr. Robert Eisler in his book *The Messiah Jesus and John the Baptist* (Methuen, London,

1931), Jesus of Nazareth was actually proclaimed King shortly before the Feast, on the Mount of Olives. The insurrectionary movement swiftly spread to the Temple Courts, and when Pilate arrived in Jerusalem, rather belatedly, after a series of forced marches, he was compelled to retake by force certain vital positions which had already capitulated to the Galilean mob. Eisler's suggestion that the "Tower in Siloam", which he identifies with the southernmost point of the city wall, fell during these operations, crushing beneath it many of the insurgents, though seemingly fantastic, is too closely allied to the revolutionary theory to be dismissed summarily or without comment.

It is only right to mention here that many liberal scholars who discern traces of a revolutionary movement in the language of the Gospels reject decisively the extreme conclusions of the Jewish critic. Revolution, however, even if unsuccessful, is a formidable thing and there can be little doubt that, faced by an insurgent movement of the kind postulated, Pilate would have been compelled to act swiftly, without reference to the slow-moving and rather cumbrous machinery of the Jewish State. There could have been no half-measures in the presence of those vast crowds of excited pilgrims.

Now it is a very curious and suggestive fact that, from a purely logical standpoint, there does not seem to be any tolerable compromise between these two opposed and mutually exclusive hypotheses. It is a case either of Revolution or Sacrifice, and when once you are committed to the latter you are committed also to a view of Pilate's probable behaviour which bears a marked resemblance to that recorded in the Gospels.

In order to give Dr. Eisler's suggested reconstruction a scrupulously fair hearing, I decided to take the earliest of the Christian narratives—the Gospel according to St. Mark—and submit the facts recorded therein to a series of critical and highly objective tests. This study will be found to occupy the greater part of the space at our disposal. Indeed, it was in the main the work which I went out to do.

From this threefold line of inquiry there emerged slowly a portrait of the Roman Procurator which revealed him to be, if not an heroic, at least a consistent and intelligible figure. The ancient scene, magically preserved for us in the pages of Josephus and the New Testament, had come to life. Regretfully, in imagination, I saw him re-embark—a sad and disillusioned man—to face the last dread summons of his Emperor.

And then an unexpected thing happened. . . .

My work in Jerusalem was completed and I was standing one evening in the Palm Court of the King David Hotel, watching by moonlight that unforgettable skyline which stretches from the black mass of the Citadel to the tall white tower of the Dormition Church on the south-west hill. The night was very still, and through the gap in the hills which leads down through Bethany to Jericho I saw the ghostly outline of the mountains of Moab. Save that the walls were loftier and stretched farther to the south, just such a scene might a Judean shepherd, tending his flock on the high ground near the Mamilla pool, have witnessed on the night when Pilate set sail from Caesarea.

Suddenly I remembered that the date was A.D. 36, and that in the summer of that year the Apostle Paul, fresh from his solitary communing in the Arabian desert, had spent an entire fortnight in the city. Instinctively my eye sought the point in the dark wall behind which an hour earlier, as the daylight faded, I had noted the inconspicuous dome which marks the site of the Caenaculum. Somewhere near that spot, I reflected, must have stood the house with the Upper Room—and to this Paul, now a converted Christian, would surely go. Could there be any place more sacred to him than that revered room in which Jesus had instituted the sacrament of the Last Supper? Yes, I was pretty certain that the resident apostles would take him there!

Equally instinctively, I measured with my eye the distance which separates this room from the reputed site of the Holy Sepulchre. It is amazingly short. You could traverse it in six minutes. I asked myself quite plainly whether it was a tolerable proposition that the man who ultimately wrote the fifteenth chapter of the First Letter to the Corinthians could have stayed *fourteen days in Jerusalem and not once have made that short journey.* If he did, what were his emotions as he stood close to the place where, according to our modernistic interpretations, his great Leader was sleeping His last sleep?

It is a hard question, but God knows that in that spot at least I was in no mood for illusions.

Then, slowly, there came back to me, point by point, the whole massive case for the story of the women's visit to the tomb, as it is described in that very primitive document, the Gospel according to St. Mark, and, more for the sake of my own peace of mind than for any other reason, I sat down there and then and wrote the Postscript which is appended to this volume.

The historical student may, if he wishes, disregard it altogether. But if his interest extends to the subject of which it treats he will find therein some considerations which I have not explicitly stated elsewhere. Who shall say that, even on a rationalistic interpretation of the facts, the events of that Easter morning were not the most considerable events of the period which we are now about to study?

5. THE SO–CALLED "HOUSE OF PILATE"
Built in the eleventh or twelfth century from much more ancient material.
Probably the scene of the "Trial" in the old Roman procession plays repre-
senting the Passion

6. IN SEARCH OF PILATE'S ROME

The Piazza del Popolo, showing the famous obelisk from Heliopolis, first erected in the Circus Maximus about the year B.C. 10

CHAPTER III

THE ROMAN PARADOX

WHAT do we really know about Pontius Pilate and his wife, Claudia, prior to that memorable decade which they spent in Judea and Samaria?

I asked myself the question as the great Imperial Airways flying-boat "Challenger", after a record run from Southampton to Marseilles, lifted herself from the blue waters of Lake Marignane and set her course for the Eternal City. I had to admit that we know very little. History is curiously silent concerning that early and very significant period.

There are, of course, many legends.

The Italian historian, Rosadi, expresses the belief that Pilate came from Seville—one of the four cities of Spain which enjoyed the right of Roman citizenship—and that his wife, Claudia Procula, was a Gaul. I can find no adequate basis for this tradition. Eusebius who gives some interesting facts concerning Pilate, does not deal with his early life at all and the Christian Fathers are also silent upon this point. It looks as though historical interest in the Roman Procurator arose too late in the

Christian era for the casual allusions to his early career to rest upon fact.

It is widely believed, however, that the name *Pontius* gives a possible clue and that Pilate was of Samnite descent. It was a Samnite general, Pontius, who inflicted upon the Roman legions the humiliation of surrender at the Caudine Forks, and the name frequently occurs in Roman literature after the Samnites themselves had been defeated and absorbed. Among the contemporaries of Julius Caesar appears the name of one Lucius Pontius Aquila, a friend of Cicero. It is possible that Pontius Pilate may have been a member of one of these Samnite families.

On the other hand, a persistent tradition runs through the medieval literature of southern Germany that Pilate was born in a little village named Forscheim, in the Mayence Canton on the left bank of the Rhine. This was definitely stated in the twelfth century and it derives considerable support from the folk-lore and poetry of the German peoples.

The legend, which has many interesting variants, attributes the birth of Pilate to the union of Tyrus, the King of a semi-Romanized tribe, with a miller's daughter who did not, of course, rank as his consort or queen.

Late one evening—so the medieval story runs—King Tyrus, after a day's hunting in the district now known as Berteich in the Mayence country, became detached from his followers and lost his way. He looked to the heavens for guidance, and perceived an unusual constellation. "A male child, begotten this night, will have

fame or infamy greater than that of any other mortal"—
such was the augury which he read in the stars. The
King pressed on in an effort to reach shelter, and by the
light of the moon came to Pila's mill where he was
received with fitting honours. Tyrus was about to settle
for the night on the bearskins when the miller's daughter,
a young and attractive maiden, brought in the great
garlanded drinking horn—the good-night libation.
"Fetch old Drude," commanded the now passionate
monarch. "I will wed this girl at once so that the gods'
augury may be fulfilled." It would seem that the aged
priestess was conveniently near, for within an hour the
ceremony was performed and in due time a boy, Pilate,
was born.

The same legend asserts that the youthful Pilate,
during the course of a quarrel, killed his half-brother,
the King's legitimate son, and that soon after this mis-
deed he was sent as a hostage to Rome where he was
accepted as the King's natural son and secured the
favour of the Emperor Augustus.

All this, of course, is of very doubtful authenticity.

The earliest traditions are removed by centuries from
the time of the events and even the military and political
antecedents of Pilate are obscure. It is clear, however,
that at some time he must have been made a knight,
since only those of equestrian rank could hold the procuratorship. There are also allusions in the literature to
his having served under Germanicus in Germany and
to an administrative period in Pontus.

Perhaps the most trustworthy of the scant and often contradictory traditions about Pilate is that he received his appointment to Judea on the recommendation of Sejanus. It is significant that the year in which Pilate set out to relieve Valerius Gratus, his predecessor, was also the year in which Tiberius relinquished his active control of affairs in Rome and retired to the island of Capri. Sejanus, as the Emperor's principal minister and trusted deputy, was at this period at the zenith of his power. Notoriously hostile to the Jews, this subtle and ambitious courtier may well have thought that Pilate's brusque and self-assertive manner rendered him the ideal man to control that turbulent people. . . .

But here we are, at last, at Lake Bracciano, the *Lacus Sabatinus* of antiquity. The lowered pitch of our propellers tells us that we are about to descend and in a few minutes we are safely moored close to the little town of Anguillara on the lake-side. A dilapidated sign-post informs us that Rome is thirty-five kilometres distant. Conveniently a car awaits us on the quay and after a pleasant run of about fifty minutes we cross the Tiber at the Ponte Milvio. It was here that the Emperor Maxentius, fleeing to the river after his decisive defeat by Constantine the Great, was drowned. So we enter Rome by one of her historic approaches, the Flaminian Way.

An abrupt stop at one of the innumerable traffic lights warns us that we are now in the busy heart of a great metropolis. Already the hour is late and the long, narrow canyon of the Corso Umberto is brilliantly outlined by neon signs. The air is laden with petrol vapour, and as our car draws to the kerb in a quiet street at the foot of the Pincian hill we are glad of the comfort and respite which our hotel can offer. Pilate will not run away! To-morrow we can start our investigation amid the authentic archaeological remains of his own time.

And yet, when the opportunity does come to explore Rome quietly and at our leisure we shall have to admit that, in a direct and personal sense, the historical Pilate eludes us.

I remember that Mr. H. V. Morton had a similar experience. In his very interesting book, *In the Steps of St. Paul*, he describes how, on arriving by train late one evening, he rang up a friend and explained that on this occasion he was interested only in Rome of the first century, the Rome which St. Paul had known. He received a rather disconcerting reply:

> Then, my friend, very little above ground exists for you. St. Peter's does not exist. St. John Lateran does not exist. The Vatican Museum does not exist. Even the Colosseum does not exist. My friend, you have come to see the *cellars* of Rome.

It was an exaggeration, of course, but if it be approximately true of the great Apostle of the Gentiles it applies with double force to the Roman Procurator. Not even the cellars of Rome disclose any real consciousness on the part of his contemporaries of the future significance of Pilate in the spiritual and political history of the world. It is as though he had never lived, so devoid is the capital of any assured tradition concerning him.

There is indeed one building, near the Temple of Vesta, in the older part of the city, to which the uninstructed visitor may be directed and which is often described to-day as the House of Pilate. Actually, it is over a thousand years too late!

Despite the ancient materials used in its construction, it is generally believed to have been built by one of the Crescentii family in the eleventh or twelfth century. A tradition which associates this house with Rienzi, the famous Italian reformer, and the last of the tribunes, is probably without foundation.

We are compelled, therefore, to look elsewhere.

Perhaps the best way to sense the atmosphere of ancient Rome, as Pilate knew it, is to take a walk in the clear Italian sunshine, as I did one lovely spring morning, and to pick out those things of assured antiquity which it is quite certain were familiar objects to the citizens of that far-off day.

It is surprising how numerous they are.

You cannot do better than begin your pilgrimage in the Piazza del Popolo, at the foot of the Pincian hill, and look across the great square towards the entrance to the Corso Umberto, jealously guarded by its twin churches.

Already you are gazing at something which must have been very familiar to Pontius Pilate—the great obelisk which points its graceful needle to the skies in the centre of the Piazza. It did not then stand, as it does now, on the central line of the Via Latia—at that time a narrow thoroughfare through which cattle, horses, mules, wine-carts, soldiers, farmers and provincials jostled their way from the north into the heart of Rome. But the obelisk was ancient and venerable even in Republican times. Pliny tells us that the Emperor Augustus, after his decisive defeat of Mark Antony at the battle of Actium, transported it from Heliopolis, the now ruined city at the head of the Nile delta, and caused it to be set up in the Circus Maximus at Rome. Pilate was then about twelve years old. The year was B.C. 10. Here it certainly stood throughout the Procurator's lifetime and for many centuries thereafter.[1]

As a soldier and a member of the equestrian order, Pilate must often have attended the military spectacles and games held in the Circus, and the Egyptian obelisk, with its unfamiliar inscriptions, can hardly have failed to summon to his mind a picture of the strange country which the skill and valour of Augustus had brought once more under the Roman sway. Little, perhaps, did he realize that a few years later he would set foot on Egyptian soil and travel thence to an even stranger outpost of the Empire.

Another impressive survival of the Augustan age lies a short distance away in the Corso Umberto, near which stands the Augusteo, the immense circular mausoleum of the Emperor Augustus—until recently a concert hall,

---

[1] At some unknown period the obelisk fell down and it remained partially buried until A.D. 1589, when it was recovered by Sixtus V and re-erected on its present site by the celebrated architect, Domenico Fontana.

35

but now cleared of the mean buildings which surrounded it, and put to more decorative uses.

This gloomy and austere relic is a place of crowded memories.

When Pilate left Rome in A.D. 26 the mausoleum was but fifty-four years old and was thus a comparatively recent addition to the city. Yet already it was the tomb of many famous contemporaries. Marcellus, "the pride and hope of Rome", Marcus Agrippa, Octavia, Germanicus, Drusus, were all buried here and, of course, the divine Augustus himself, whose body, in Tacitus's memorable phrase, was burnt on so huge a pyre that his wife, Livia, "watched it for five days and nights before it was cool enough for her to collect the imperial ashes".

Twenty-three years later, Pontius Pilate, having received the dread summons to return to Rome to answer in person the accusation of his enemies, must have found some consolation in the fact that, on reaching the capital, the man at whose imperious command he had been recalled from Judea was safely buried in this forbidding tomb.

But, of course, the place where the memories crowd thickest, and the outlines of temples and palaces, long buried, speak with a certain quiet authority of those far-off days, is the Forum. This surely is the most magical archaeological preserve in the whole world. Forgotten are the bustling streets, the electric signs, the cinemas and cafés of the modern city. It is as though they did not exist.

7. OVERLOOKING THE FORUM

Showing the Temple of Saturn and the Arch of Septimius Severus from the site of the ancient Tabularium

8. "TU ES PETRUS"

Part of the famous inscription under the Dome of St. Peter's at Rome

Some of these vast buildings, now reduced to ruins, did not, of course, stand here in Pilate's day. The noble Arch of Titus, with its sculptured frieze commemorating the siege and capture of Jerusalem, was not erected until A.D. 81. The once magnificent Basilica of Constantine, the Golden House of Nero, the Arch of Septimius Severus, and beyond, the mighty ellipse of the Colosseum— dominating its site as no other ancient amphitheatre has ever done—belong to later days. But in the quiet of this secluded spot one can reconstruct in imagination much of the city which Pilate knew.

Here is the Tarpeian Rock, its long history still clouded by legend. Here also is the famous Tabularium, the Record Office of the Caesars. Near by, deep down beneath the foundations of a later Christian church, lies the dreaded and gloomy dungeon of the Mamertine Prison, originally a well-house, but converted later to more sinister uses. Sallust speaks of it in terms almost of terror.

The ancient streets which intersect the Forum, with their rich complex of ruined buildings, still speak to us of the architectural glories which made the city famous throughout the Graeco-Roman world. Few modern thoroughfares can boast a more impressive façade than that, for example, which formed the south side of the Via Sacra, beginning with the Temple of Saturn—the Public Treasury of Rome—and terminating with the slender grace and beauty of the temple of the twin-gods, Castor and Pollux. Between these, and separated from them by two busy streets, stood the magnificent Basilica Julia, founded by Julius Caesar and rebuilt by Augustus after a disastrous fire.

On the opposite side of the Forum, facing this splendid line of public offices and in a sense rivalling their magnificence, rose the great Basilica Aemilia, one of the finest structures in Rome, which had many vicissitudes and, as its present condition testifies, finally went up in flames. Innumerable pieces of melted iron and bronze, with a number of small coins, still adhere firmly to the marble flooring.

Other buildings, contemporary with Pilate, of which some vestiges remain are: the triumphal arch of Tiberius (built in A.D. 17 to commemorate the recovery of the Roman Eagles lost by Varus seven years earlier); the Temples of Augustus, Julius Caesar and the goddess Vesta; the House of the Vestal Virgins; the *Sacellum Cloacina*; and, at the western approach to the Forum, close to the ancient Comitium, the great Temple of Concordia, long used for meetings of the Senate and later a museum of Greek art.

If the little stump, close to the Temple of Saturn, known as the *Milarium Aureum*, really is the base of the Golden Milestone we can be fairly certain that Pilate frequently lingered here, since there were inscribed upon it in letters of gold the distances to the more important cities of the Empire.

Finally, a short walk will take us to the foot of the Palatine hill, from the summit of which, surrounded by the ruins of the great palaces and temples of the Caesars, we can look down upon the modern Via dei Cerchi and the outline (still traceable) of the Circus Maximus.

Such was the heart of Rome as it existed in that memorable year when Tiberius, in a fit of petulance and disillusionment, relinquished his active control of affairs in the capital and retired to the seclusion of Capri.

Round about this maze of buildings the new Procurator must have spent some busy days preparing for his journey to Judea. He could hardly leave Italy for a long period without first disposing of his own personal and private interests. There would be State business to transact; friends to visit in the various public offices, and at least one journey up the winding street of the Palatine to the Domus Tiberiana, where he probably received his final instructions in person from his imperial master.

Then, as spring came round—the period of fair winds and comparatively swift travel—we can imagine him setting out, accompanied by his chosen officers and his wife, Claudia, for the coast. By descending the Palatine hill to the south-east corner of the Circus Maximus, close to the present church of Saint Gregory the Great, we can watch him go.

Somewhere here stood the ancient Porta Capena in the Servian wall, from which issued the immemorial highroad, the Appian Way. It is a morning in A.D. 26. There is the usual congestion in the narrow stone-

39

flagged streets as men and beasts wait their turn to pass through the narrow portal. Suddenly the sound of an approaching cavalcade is heard and a Roman officer steps forward and clears the way as the Governor and his consort, accompanied by their escort, pass through. Gravely the officer salutes. There is a buzz of excited conversation, then slowly the clatter of hoofs and the rumble of wheels upon the highway die away. A few moments later the Procurator and his little cavalcade disappear in a cloud of dust on their way to the coast. Presently we shall follow them.

Meanwhile we have some business to transact on the opposite bank of the Tiber.

Nineteen centuries have passed and, as we retrace our steps towards the centre of the city, the pagan temples and the Caesarean palaces dissolve behind us in decay. We are back in modern Rome. The cafés, the cinemas, the electric signs, the noisy trams and the raucous motor-buses are with us again. A broad new street brings us to the Ponte Vittorio Emmanuel and thus to the Borgo, the ancient Anglo-Saxon settlement on the farther bank of the river.

The long, low ridge of the Janiculum looms ahead, at the foot of which Caligula and Nero had a circus of evil memory. We are reminded of it as we cross the vast Piazza di San Pietro, with its massive colonnades of Tuscan pillars, and give a passing glance to the great obelisk of Thothmes III which stands at its centre. This is the only Egyptian obelisk which remained erect in

Rome throughout the Dark Ages. It was brought by
Caligula from Heliopolis and was set up in the adjoining
circus, where it stood, a silent and impenetrable witness,
throughout the frightful orgies of Nero's reign. In A.D.
1586 it was removed by Domenico Fontana to its present
site.

So we mount the broad steps leading to the vestibule
of the great Cathedral of St. Peter.

It is an impressive moment for the visitor when he
passes for the first time into a church which for sheer
vastness and for the wealth of its religious associations
has no parallel throughout the world. To those who
know the Duomo in Florence, the Sistine Chapel, and
many a lovely shrine of lesser proportions, it will seem
at first, perhaps, to lack warmth and colour, but the
mood soon passes in the presence of a certain timeless
majesty which can awe and thrill even the least sensitive
spirit. It is as though these massive pillars, like the
Parthenon at Athens, stood eternally founded upon rock.
One can imagine Pontius Pilate and his wife, who saw
Herod's temple in Jerusalem in all its glory, standing
to-day in the nave of this great building and feeling it
not unworthy of their own Imperial Rome.

And then suddenly, as we look up into the misty
cupola with its famous mosaics lost in gloom, we begin
to become conscious of a very startling fact. Around the
base of the dome, in letters of blue upon a gold mosaic
background, are written these words:

TU ES PETRUS, ET SUPER HANC PETRAM AEDIFICABO ECCLESIAM MEUM, ET TIBI DABO CLAVES REGNI CAELORUM.[1]

Something tells us that we are standing here in the presence of a tremendous paradox. The intervening centuries are forgotten and from that high dome there seems to come down to us the very laughter of the Gods.

Who was this Petrus whose name is thus emblazoned in the place of peculiar honour beneath the mighty dome of this ancient and venerable fane? He was a simple fisherman from the shores of Galilee, originally known to his friends as Simon Barjona. How he ultimately came to be called Peter is another story, but on that memorable Friday morning in April, A.D. 29, when Pilate faced the biggest crisis of his life; when the great square before the Praetorium was a sea of angry faces and when tumultuous throngs swept through the narrow streets of Jerusalem towards the gates, Simon was hiding in a house within a short distance of all that turmoil, unnerved and shaken, ashamed even of the very name he bore.

Who also was he who is reputed to have declared in this confident and emphatic manner that *upon the rock of this man's character* he would build a church and would give to him the keys of the Kingdom of Heaven? We shall meet him presently upon the steps of the Prae-

[1] "Thou art Peter, and upon this rock I will build my church, and I will give thee the keys of the Kingdom of Heaven."

42

torium, an indicted Prisoner, a man accused (and ultimately convicted) of treason against Rome.

Yet that Prisoner and His friends—Simon, Andrew and the rest—have since covered the world with churches and have filled our libraries and museums with master-pieces innumerable. The streets of Rome to-day proclaim their triumph from every corner. As for Pilate, you will find him only in the shadows, a sort of literary phantom, a misty recollection and a name.

CHAPTER IV

EASTWARD BOUND

We know from St. Luke's classic description of the ship-wreck of St. Paul that crossing the Mediterranean Sea in the first century was a somewhat perilous undertaking and the time required for such journeys varied consider-ably according to the season of the year.

Lucian tells us of a merchantman, laden with corn from Egypt, which put into the harbour at Athens seventy days after leaving Alexandria. On the other hand, news of Galba's succession is known to have reached the Egyptian seaport within twenty-seven days, a feat which was, perhaps, only possible during the spring and summer months when the outward passage was favoured by the Etesian winds.

It would thus take Pilate roughly two months to travel from his apartments in Rome to his official residence in Caesarea. He would almost certainly break his journey at Alexandria, where he would probably meet Valerius Gratus, the retiring Governor, and make the acquain-tance of the more influential members of the large Jewish colony in that City.

9. AN ARTIST'S IMPRESSION
of the Tower of Pharos, regarded by the ancients as one of the Seven
Wonders of the World. From the top of this tower "a fire was exhibited
to such as sailed to Alexandria"

10. ENTRANCE TO THE JUDEAN HILLS

The Jaffa Road beginning its long climb from the Maritime Plain to the
gates of the City

Other and more personal considerations may also have detained him. As the finest mart in the Orient and a great centre of cosmopolitan culture, Alexandria must have presented an irresistible attraction to his wife Claudia. Here in the gay bazaars of Cleopatra's city she could most conveniently replenish her wardrobe and prepare for her long stay in the comparatively inhospitable regions of Judea and Samaria. Later a coastal ship would take the Procurator and his party to Caesarea.

Compare this leisurely progress with the swifter and more convenient travel of to-day.

We in our luxurious flying-boat, propelled by four mighty 950 h.p. engines, can make the journey from Rome to Alexandria in about nine hours. From here, if we are in a hurry, one of the giant land-planes of the Misr Airways will take us to Lydda in one hour and fifty minutes. It sounds fantastic—as indeed it is. When I mentioned these facts to an old Bedouin on the desolate beach at Ascalon, he looked at me with strange and puzzled eyes. The true Oriental does not readily conceive distances in miles or kilometres. He thinks spontaneously in terms of what a Western statistician would call *camel-hours* and to this simple son of the desert there were innumerable camel-hours between Rome and Lydda.

With this magical gift of swift transport at our disposal I suggest, therefore, to the reader that we should leave Pilate's sail-crowded barque ploughing the seas round the dangerous Attic coast and go on ahead.

This will give us an opportunity to study in advance certain characteristics of the Judean landscape which have an important bearing upon our problem. There is plenty of time. The Procurator and his party have still many leagues of treacherous sea before them.

Alexandria, then, is our first objective.

It is a morning in early spring, and dawn is just breaking over the Alban hills as our car sweeps silently across a deserted Piazza del Popolo and takes once again the historic highway to the north. Few people are about and a light mist obscures the valleys as we traverse the long winding road to Lake Bracciano. At Anguillara they are opening the shutters to greet another day of warm and brilliant sunshine. On the lake itself activity prevails. The second officer is "revving" up the engines of the flying boat, and as we step from the open tender on to the gangway there is a welcome smell of hot coffee. Appetites are keen on this lovely fresh spring morning and the steward is determined to justify his culinary reputation.

In a few minutes we are seated. There is a mighty roar from the engines and two great welts of spray drench our windows. Slowly the flying-boat detaches itself from the impeding waters of the lake and banks steeply over the now ridiculously tiny figures watching us from the shore. Shall we miss the tops of those gaunt crags which rise so threateningly behind the lake? Apparently we shall, for we are now climbing fast and the Apennines with their snow-clad peaks lie ahead.

I suppose that few travellers will dispute that the

journey by air from Rome to Alexandria, made in the early spring under ideal conditions, is one of the most entrancing single-day flights in the world and the traveller must be strangely unimaginative if he is not moved to deep reflection by it.

Once you have crossed the Apennines (the altimeter here registers between ten and eleven thousand feet) the worst of your troubles are over and the machine glides gently down into the spacious harbour at Brindisi. If you are as lucky as we were, you will be refreshed with tea in the Customs House while the Italian officials complete their formalities.

From here the journey to Athens is a sheer delight.

Hardly have you left Brindisi before the snowcapped peaks of the Albanian mountains come into view. You leave these to the north-east and head straight for the island of Corfu—the ancient Scheria—where Homer tells us King Alcinous reigned. You get a passing view of the picturesque little harbour as the ship crosses the northern extremity of the island. In half an hour, still skirting the Greek coast, you are over the Gulf of Arta, a deep inlet of the sea almost enclosed by its own headlands, at the southern extremity of which stands Actium, the scene of Octavian's victory over the combined fleets of Antony and Cleopatra. From a height of five thousand feet with the blue unruffled waters of the bay beneath you, it is difficult to realize that the most decisive naval battle of antiquity took place just outside this spacious natural harbour.

On fine days the flying-boat here crosses the mainland and comes out ultimately over a long stretch of sea, hemmed in to the north and south by high mountains. The trail of ships passing in both directions tells us that we are following one of the great highways of the world. A tongue of land ahead seems to bar its further progress until we observe that an artificial canal, cut through the isthmus, joins our highway with the open sea beyond.

Close to the entrance of the canal, far beneath us, is a collection of brown roofs and when realization fully comes we get our first thrill. For this is Corinth!

As the "Challenger" approached the isthmus, Captain Woodhouse, knowing my quest, sent down word from the cockpit that he was slightly changing his course so that we might fly directly over the ancient city. I went to the window and as I looked down upon the unfolding of that amazing panorama, I seemed to see in one of those houses an oldish bandy-legged man pacing the floor and dictating eagerly to his scribe Tertius what has since been recognized as one of the greatest pieces of sustained writing in the world. There came floating up to me from those brown roofs the actual and memorable words in which he addressed himself to his friends in Rome and Ephesus:

> Paul, a servant of Jesus Christ . . . to all that are at Rome . . . grace to you and peace from God our Father and the Lord Jesus Christ . . . I commend unto you Phoebe our sister, who is a servant of the church that is at Cenchreae; that you receive her in the Lord, worthily of the saints, and

that ye assist her in whatsoever matter she may have need of you: for she herself also hath been a succourer of many and of mine own self . . . Timothy my fellow-worker saluteth you; and Lucius and Jason and Sosipater, my kinsman. Gaius my host, and of the whole church, saluteth you. Erastus the treasurer of the city saluteth you and Quartus the brother. Tertius also, who transcribes this epistle, salutes you in the Lord.

What a glimpse this famous passage gives us of the many-sided human interests of those early Christian days. My heart went out to that sturdy and valiant old fighter as our ship, with the wings of an eagle, sped across the isthmus and Corinth faded from our view.

In less than half an hour the flying-boat descends upon the waters of the Saronian Gulf in full view of the Acropolis at Athens. No! You are not going to land! We stop here merely to take up petrol and to receive and discharge passengers. Then, after exchanging greetings with our Greek hosts, we set off upon the long flight across the Mediterranean. The lovely islands of the Cyclades, their glistening white rocks crowned by trees of vivid green, pass swiftly beneath us. Presently the island of Crete with its forbidding range of dark limestone mountains looms ahead. It lies directly across our path. If you are very lucky and the ship needs petrol, the pilot will bring you down into the adorable little harbour at Mirabella Bay, one of the most enchanting spots in the Mediterranean. Here the Imperial Airways depot ship has her base and, for a short time while the tankers are at work, you will enjoy the Captain's hospitality, served in the cosy cabin of the "Imperia".

With a great roar we are off again, climbing steeply to cross the island. The Lassithi Mountains are soon lost to view and for the next three or four hours no land is in sight. Tea is served in the saloon and then, almost imperceptibly, the golden sands of Egypt, reflecting the glory of the afternoon sun, appear as a thin but conspicuous line upon the horizon. The steward, emerging from his fastness in the fore of the boat, amid the tinkle of crockery, observes almost casually: "Alexandria in twenty minutes." It sounds incredible, but our ship is sweeping forward at 150 miles an hour. In a few minutes the vast mosaic of the Egyptian seaport, with its narrow streets and crowded bazaars, lies beneath us. We bank steeply and describe a huge circle to gain position and lose height for the final run up the harbour. As we do so, the lighthouse of Ras-el-Tin, standing at the end of the claw-like promontory which guards the inner harbour—queerly tilted by reason of the angle of the boat— glides past our window.

It is then, I think, that the student of history gets his greatest thrill, because that beacon stands close to the spot where, thousands of years ago, there stood what was probably the first and certainly the most famous lighthouse in the world.

The rocky base upon which it rests is all that remains of the once famous island of Pharos. In the days of the Phoenician sea-rovers it was a haunt of pirates and many a hard-pressed mariner sought refuge in the sheltered waters which lay behind it. Homer, in the Odyssey, has left us a vivid picture of the scene:

> Upon the surging ocean wave there lies a rocky isle,
> 'Tis Pharos called, which stands against the opening of
>   the Nile,
> So far as in a single day a hollow ship may fare,
> If on her sheet the whistling wind shall favourably bear.
> Behind the island is a port where galleys ride secure,
> Until, their watery load baled out, they venture forth
>   once more.

Upon the eastern extremity of this islet Ptolemy II erected a great tower upon the top of which a light burned continuously. Josephus speaks of it in the Antiquities as "The Tower of Pharus . . . which exhibited a fire to such as sailed to Alexandria".

This famous structure, known to the ancients as the "Third Wonder of the World", was frequently depicted upon the coins of the period. It was about 400 feet in height and was connected with the mainland by a causeway which terminated in a viaduct rising upon arches of increasing height. The whole conception was the work of the distinguished architect and engineer, Sostratus of Cnidus.

The flame was produced by burning resinous wood upon the cylindrical platform which crowned the edifice, and it is believed that metal mirrors were used to increase the range of the beacon which could normally be seen by mariners from a distance of about thirty kilometres. It is an impressive thought that as their tiny ship buffeted its way through the darkness towards the Egyptian coast,

Pilate and Claudia must have seen that welcome and reassuring light.

There is, however, another and a far more intimate point of contact with our subject in this vast cosmopolitan seaport. It was the home, throughout his long life, of the philosopher, Philo, a man of wide culture and learning, whose voluminous writings can still be read with profit and understanding to-day.

Now our special interest in Philo of Alexandria is two-fold. In the first place he was strictly contemporary with Pontius Pilate, having been born between the years 10 and 20 B.C. The two men were therefore about the same age and Philo was almost certainly resident in Alexandria when the Procurator first visited the city in A.D. 26.

Secondly, Philo clearly held Pilate in very marked contempt. His indignation towards the Roman Governor knew no bounds and in a classic passage he pours the vials of his wrath upon him, denouncing him unsparingly:

> in respect of his corruption, his acts of insolence, his rapine, his habit of insulting people, his cruelty, his continual murders of people untried and uncondemned, his never-ending, gratuitous and most grievous inhumanity.

Whether that furious onslaught was justified by the facts is a matter which, later, we shall have to consider very closely.

Unfortunately there is very little in modern Alexandria to stimulate our imagination or to recall the glories of the past. The spacious and well-planned city which

Alexander the Great founded in B.C. 332, and which the Ptolemies enriched with noble buildings, has suffered many vicissitudes since its great library (later destroyed by fire) was universally recognized as the cultural metropolis of the ancient world. To-day, the place is little more than a vast commercial seaport, a centre of barter and exchange, a necessary link between the sea-ways of the Mediterranean and the land routes through Egypt and the Orient. We shall therefore take the earliest opportunity to continue our journey.

Two courses are open to us. One is to fly along the coast to the little desert landing-ground at Port Said, one of the most romantic and stimulating of the smaller airports in the world. Here we can await the arrival of the daily air-liner which runs from Cairo to Lydda. By this route you can have breakfast in Alexandria and lunch on the same day in your hotel in Jerusalem.

The other is to take the Egyptian State Railway across the now cultivated flats of the Nile Delta to El-Kantara on the Suez Canal. Here a convenient ferryboat will convey the traveller to Kantara East where a familiar wagon-lit attached to the Jerusalem express awaits him. The train starts shortly after midnight and since the greater part of the journey is necessarily made under cover of darkness, we shall choose the swifter and more convenient route.

The flight from Alexandria to Port Said affords a wonderful panoramic view of the great lakes and the two divergent arms of the Nile making respectively for their outlets at the Rosetta and Dalmietta mouths. The plane lands upon the dry sand of the desert. For a few minutes bustle and activity prevail as our baggage is unloaded and the great Cairo-Haifa four-engined liner comes into sight. The monstrous bird alights and a few bored and sophisticated travellers, due to rejoin their ship for Suez and the East, descend the gangway. We are shown into their places and with little more fuss than that experienced when a long-distance train stops at a suburban station, the machine soars into the air and we are off on the last hop of our long journey.

The Suez Canal, straight as a die, with its burden of great ships bound for inconceivably remote places, fades swiftly to a thin and almost imperceptible pencil line across the map of Egypt. Eastward, as far as the eye can reach, the desert stretches; to the south an arid wilderness rising gently to the foothills of the mighty Sinaitic range; to the north, close in, almost beneath us, the white fringe of the Mediterranean laps the low-lying shore.

As though sensing our eagerness to sight the Promised Land, the machine changes direction and pulls out boldly across the waves. We are cutting out the long sweep of the coast in this almost forsaken corner of the Inland Sea. A few minutes more and the sandy fringe of the Philistine plain is in sight. We cross it close to the ruins of ancient Ascalon, now but a memory of its former and historic self. The railway and the Gaza road slip beneath us. To the east, the sullen outline of the Judean

54

hills, with their stony treeless heights, affords a strange contrast to the plain beneath us which is richly planted with groves in which oranges, lemons and grapefruit grow in profusion. Indeed, so fascinated are we by this luxurious growth that we fail to notice a star-shaped white pattern in the open space beyond. This is the concrete runway of the Lydda aerodrome, flanked by its finely appointed and comfortable buildings. The pitch of the propellers sinks to an almost inaudible whirr as we glide down and taxi into port.

We are now about thirty-one miles from Jerusalem, and by the forethought of our hotel a private car will be awaiting us. The Customs formalities are quickly over and, after stowing our luggage, an Arab driver, attired incongruously in a Western lounge suit and a red tarboosh, takes the wheel. The roads are hedged with cactus and the air is filled with the scent of ripe fruit as we slip past Lydda towards Ramleh. The car slows down as we approach a junction. Major road ahead! This is the Jerusalem-Jaffa highway, one of the busiest through-routes in Palestine, and we must make our entrance cautiously. Private vehicles, armoured cars, military lorries, heavily laden camels and asses share this great artery.

A mobile policeman, followed by a big limousine bearing the arms of the High Commissioner, stridently announce from behind their intention to overtake, and sweep by on a long, straight stretch of the road. But we are in no mood to reach our destination in so precipitate a manner. Familiarity has not yet hardened us to the

wonders of the journey. There is not an inch of this
great highway which is not of interest to the pilgrim. I
have travelled along it many times, but never without
a strange uplifting of the spirit.

Shortly after leaving Ramleh the railway to Jerusalem
crosses our road, and to the right we get our first glimpse
of the low mound of Gezer, a city once held by the
Egyptians, which was given as a dowry by the reigning
Pharaoh to his daughter upon her marriage to Solomon.
The place is mentioned in the Tell-el-Armarna Tablets
and much interesting excavation has already taken place.
Presently a minor road branches to the left and an inconspicuous sign-post tells us that it leads to the Valley of
Ajalon, where Joshua fought one of his most decisive
battles. Ahead are the low, soft hills of the Shephelah,
with the fierce crags of the Judean heights rising steeply
behind. Somewhere upon the crest of those mountains
Jerusalem stands.

The country now becomes wilder and more rugged.
The intensive cultivation ceases and at the little village
of Bab-el-Wad, with its Police Post, we come to the
Gateway to the Hills—a rocky pass through which our
car starts its long climb to the capital. This is an adorable
little spot of quiet natural beauty with some promise of
the grandeur beyond.

Our driver changes gear to negotiate the incline, and
we climb slowly up the picturesque valley to the village
of Qaryat-el-Inab, known to the Arabs as the Village of
Grapes. It is commonly called Abu Ghosh from the name

of its Sheikh who terrorized the surrounding country about a century ago. A rough but negotiable motor track leads from this village, past Biddu and the ancient Emmaus, to the windy heights of *Nebi Samwil*, one of the loftiest points in Palestine, from which a superb view is obtained of the Maritime Plain and of the Judean range as far south as Frank Mountain.

It is said that Richard Cœur-de-Lion, standing upon this spot, and thwarted of his purpose by dissensions in his own ranks, covered his face with his shield, exclaiming: "Ah! Lord God, I pray that I may never see Thy Holy City if so be that I may not rescue it from the hands of Thine enemies."

We are now nearing the climax of our journey, for within three miles we crest the hill and there opens before us the great Beit Hanina Valley, a vast chasm down the steep sides of which the road descends with numerous hairpin bends. At the foot of the valley a broad stone bridge crosses a torrent and the road climbs again with many tortuous windings to the lofty plateau on which Jerusalem stands. Looking across this deep valley to those impressive heights we understand, perhaps for the first time, why in Biblical days people always spoke of "going *up* to Jerusalem". Nowhere, save on the approach from Jericho, is the astonishing elevation of the city more vividly realized than from this point.

Cautiously we descend the well-banked road to the level of the stream, where the ruins of some Roman buildings recall the days when ex-soldiers of the Tenth

Legion established a colony in this place. Then, climbing the opposite side of the valley, past the village of Lifta, we turn a corner and already are running into the straggling northern suburbs of Jerusalem.

To some people this sudden confrontation by the least attractive side of the ancient city is a disappointment—a sort of anticlimax to the impressive grandeur of the approach. I do not personally feel this to be the case. The visitor cannot learn too quickly that there are two quite incompatible elements in the Jerusalem which he has travelled so far to see. One is the modern outgrowth, limited to the northern and north-western sides, which is Occidental in outlook, which only time and a judicious scheme of replanning will ultimately make worthy of its unique setting. The other is that incomparable thing within the city walls, eternal, unchanging, a staggering microcosm of profound ethnographic, historic and spiritual interest.

It is one of the advantages of the approach from Jaffa that it will lead you straight to your hotel without yielding even a distant glimpse of this inner city. Yet when the mood takes you it is there, aloof and self-centred, waiting to propound to you its eternal riddles.

If you are wise you will choose the moment of that discovery with some care. For what you will see will grip you with a sense of deep and impenetrable mystery. There is a vantage point on the high ground near the Y.M.C.A. building, or better still on the terrace of the King David Hotel, whence you can see at one view a long section of the wall from David's Tower to the Dormition Church, with the Sultan's Pool lying far beneath you and the Valley of Hinnom sinking away to the great cleft which leads down to Jericho.

It is a picture which lingers in the memory, and if you feel as I did, viewing it for the first time one brilliantly sunny forenoon, you will be more conscious of its *peace and serenity* than of the tragic memories it recalls. Here is a lovely ancient thing revelling in God's sunshine on a fresh invigorating spring morning. Not a murmur reaches us of the shuffling feet within those hidden bazaars or on the narrow cobbled streets. A sort of static calm envelops the landscape, as though Time had ceased to signify and the whole scene were a sort of cross-section of Eternity.

When you have once experienced that sense of the immutability of old Jerusalem, its strange detachment from all earthly parallels, you will never lose it. Familiarity is powerless to destroy it. It is part of the spirit, the inner secret of the place.

Presently we shall enter the sombre old town and try to reconstruct at first hand the strange drama which, nearly two thousand years ago, worked itself out in those narrow winding streets. For the moment, however, our interest lies elsewhere—upon a desolate stretch of that sandy coastline which we lately glimpsed on our way to Lydda; where Jerusalem seems unreal and remote and the only sounds are the call of the seagull and the music of the waves lapping an almost forgotten shore.

CHAPTER V

THE MYSTERY OF STRATO'S TOWER

IT was a brilliantly sunny morning in early March when we paid our first visit to Caesarea.

The party consisted of four persons: my Arab driver, Lusho Fath'ullah, whom I engaged for the whole period of my stay in Palestine; Goodwin, an English guide; myself, and my wife who viewed this particular expedition with some mistrust. Only a few days earlier we had narrowly missed a bomb thrown at a Jewish bus in the Jaffa Road. The whole country was just then seething with revolt, and on the night preceding our journey a Moslem official of the Dome of the Rock had been shot in cold blood in the streets of Jerusalem. Most evenings the stillness was broken by sporadic firing.

The Military and Air Force Authorities, to whom I communicated my intentions, were not particularly encouraging. An escort from Haifa, they said—which could be spared with difficulty—might serve only to attract the attention of the bands of snipers who at that period were infesting the neighbourhood of the Carmel range. It would be better to go unobtrusively as simple

tourists. We should probably get through without difficulty. If not, as Flight-Lieut. Cummings succinctly put
it, we should "just be unlucky".

As a special concession to the occasion, Lusho Fath-
'ullah, who normally preferred to drive bare-headed,
consented to wear a tarboosh. This would at least prevent his being mistaken for a Jew.

As things turned out we had no trouble whatsoever.
Only for one instant did Goodwin's watchful eye per-
ceive danger when, over the top of a sand-dune to the
south of Caesarea, a bearded Arab appeared at the head
of a single file of about twenty followers. His anxiety
was short-lived. The menacing stranger proved to be the
local schoolmaster leading his scholars to the sea. Later
they lined up and submitted to be photographed.

The first part of the journey from Jerusalem to Caesarea
covers the familiar and much frequented highway described in the preceding chapter—the Jaffa Road.
Shortly after leaving Ramleh, with its Tower of the
Forty Martyrs—a conspicuous landmark visible for many
miles—the traveller reaches a crossing which marks
roughly his point of intersection with the historic caravan route from Egypt to Damascus. To the south lie
Gaza and the ruins of the Philistine League of Five
Cities.

Gaza itself is an unprepossessing town, shorn of the
glamour which attaches to many a place of far less
ancient lineage. Yet what strange and archaic memories
the name recalls! Here, late one night, Samson the

mighty came in secret to visit a harlot; then, outwitting his foes, escaped at midnight carrying the city gates "to the top of an hill that is before Hebron". Here, after the treachery of Delilah, they brought him, eyeless. Here, too, according to the ancient story, he pulled down the temple of Dagon upon his triumphant captors.

To-day, the Philistine stronghold is a busy little place of about 17,000 inhabitants with a small harbour hidden by sand-dunes. It is still possible to trace the course of the ancient walls. High on the hill in the centre of the upper town stand the ruins of a great mosque, originally the cathedral church of St. John. The great British cemetery, close to the station, and the aerodrome of Imperial Airways testify to the importance of the site in more recent times.

From Gaza the immemorial highway ran north, past Migdal and Isdud (the ancient Ashdod) to Lydda, whence it crossed to the pass of Megiddo, and thus gained access to the plain of Esdraelon. Standing here, upon one of the great land-bridges of the world—particularly towards evening, when the shadows fall and the rays of the dying sun gild the distant peaks of the Judean range—you can see and hear, as it were, the ghostly march of civilizations long forgotten and buried in the sand.

The phantom figures pass us in endless succession.

A spectral caravan, of the time long before Abraham, comes down from a distant gap in the Carmel range and goes slowly on its way from Babylon to Egypt. A cloud of dust in the south heralds the coming of the proud hosts of Pharaoh, carrying the dominance of Egypt to the very gates of Nineveh. Another cloud—this time in the north-east—and the bearded Assyrians upon their desert chargers thunder by. Sargon, Sennacherib, Tiglath-Pileser, Nebuchadnezzar, and many a haughty Egyptian have passed this way.

Between these sudden outbursts of martial activity the road is never silent. The endless cavalcade goes on—a sort of living frieze symbolical of all the diverse interests of the ancient world: merchant princes with their retinue carrying bales of costly fabrics; couriers between contending empires; embassies, fugitives, slaves; men and women bound upon every conceivable mission between the vast land-masses of Asia and Egypt. Such is the romance of this ancient causeway lying between the Mediterranean and the perilous sandswept plains of the Arabian desert.

On this occasion, however, our objective was the sea, and in about twenty minutes we were running into Tel-Aviv, so called after the Hebrew settlement established on the banks of the Euphrates during the Captivity. Opinions differ concerning the architectural merits of this great modern suburb of Jaffa. To some it is a welcome contrast to the sombre and primitive characteristics of the land. To others its ultra-modernism strikes a discordant note. Already a camel in Herzel Street or the Allenby Road seems almost as incongruous as in Fleet Street or the Haymarket. Personally, I found the place of small interest and was glad when our little Hillman nosed its way out of the traffic past Montefiore and Sarona to the north.

For some miles the road runs pleasantly through orchards which find a ready market for their products in the port of Jaffa. It was on this stretch that we suddenly discovered we had left behind in Jerusalem the hamper of provisions which we had prepared for the journey. We pulled in under a shady avenue of trees while Lusho went off to prospect. He came back about a quarter of an hour later with an armful of luscious oranges and grapefruit upon which we subsisted for the remainder of the day. With true Arab hospitality, the owner of the grove, hearing of our mishap, refused to take any payment.

From this point northward the country gradually becomes more rugged as the Plain narrows and the mountains edge their way towards the sea. Shortly before reaching Binyamina the road crosses the railway and starts its long, straight run past Tanturah and 'Athlit to the rocky base of Cape Carmel. Here we mistook our course. The map clearly showed a road to Caesarea, branching to the left. Goodwin thought he knew it, but he was thinking of Tanturah and we ran about ten miles in the direction of Haifa before we discovered our mistake.

As it turned out, the cartographer was right, but the "road" to the coast—so optimistically shown in red ink on the map—proved to be little more than a fair-weather

11. IMMEMORIAL CROSSING

The Jerusalem-Jaffa road close to the point where the ancient Caravan route from Egypt passed north to Megiddo and Damascus

12. FILM SHOT OF DONKEYS

Carrying photographic apparatus across the sandy waste from Binyamina to Caesarea

track across the loose shifting sand. In less than twenty
yards our car was bogged up to the axles and refused
to advance farther. There was a farmstead about half a
mile away and Goodwin left us in search of horse-
transport. After a delay which seemed interminable he
returned with a swarthy Bedouin who looked contemptuously at our modest little Hillman and inquired
scathingly why we had not brought a "real motor-car".

Under the broiling sun we argued and ultimately
struck a bargain. We could have two horses and a
donkey for 100 piastres. Goodwin protested that this was
still too much and I sat down on the footboard while
the argument continued. Finally they compromised at
sixty piastres, with an additional donkey thrown in.

So we crossed the sandy fringe of ancient Phoenicia—
at this point nearly six kilometres wide—and came to
Caesarea. We tethered our horses in the shade of the
Crusaders' wall and watched the sea lashing itself into
foam upon the overthrown pillars of Herod's Palace. It
was difficult to believe that within a few yards of this
desolate spot Vespasian, the soldier son of a comparatively obscure Roman moneylender, had been proclaimed
Emperor; that St. Paul had languished in a neighbouring
dungeon; that here Origen and Pamphilus had studied
and Eusebius received his first instruction in the Faith.

I looked out across the white-flecked waves to the
distant horizon beyond which lay Rome, and recalled
with a thrill that upon these self-same rocks Luke the
Physician must often have scanned the sea for the coastal

ship which was to take him and his great fellow-missioner on the first stage of their journey to the Imperial City. Then I sat down upon the overturned masonry and read once again the two classic passages in which Josephus describes the building of Caesarea.

Magically, the scene came to life.

Here was the great reef from which Herod, by submerging mighty stones, threw out the mole which was such a conspicuous feature of the harbour. The curve of the bay clearly marked the course of the sea-wall. Upon the higher ground close to what is now called the Cathedral Complex a few white stones fixed the site of the imposing Temple he erected to Rome and Caesar. Farther along the coast the remains of the open-air theatre still stared starkly at the sea, while to the southeast the outline of the vast Hippodrome, now neglected and overgrown with weeds, was clearly visible.

This, surely, was more even than we could have hoped and since no recent survey of contemporary Caesarea exists, and in the coming years much that is historically significant may disappear, I feel that it will not be inappropriate to describe here very briefly what I found.

1. The Crusader Fortress

It will be necessary, of course, for the reader to distinguish sharply between the *Roman* and the *Crusader* remains which now dominate the site. This is not really very difficult because the Crusaders, coming centuries later to the ruins of Herod's city, found it much too spacious for their needs and they built the walls of their fortress around the comparatively small part of the Roman town which adjoins the modern harbour. Actually the Crusaders' wall enclosed *less than one-tenth* of ancient Caesarea, a fact which is effectively demonstrated in the plan and in the aerial photographs which, by courtesy of the British Air Ministry, I am privileged to reproduce in these pages.

At the time of the Crusaders (twelfth and thirteenth centuries, A.D.) ancient Caesarea had, of course, long since fallen into decay. It probably reached the zenith of its fame during the early part of the fourth century. In the year A.D. 638 it was captured by the Mohammedans and thenceforward its sea-power faded and it shrank rapidly in size and importance. When, nearly five hundred years later, Baldwin the First stormed its relatively feeble defences the whole area within the ancient Roman *enceinte* was strewn with fragments of the original buildings as indeed, to a lesser extent, it is to-day.

The Crusaders put a great deal of this material to novel uses.

Finding, for example, a large number of granite pillars which had possibly formed part of Herod's palace, ready to their hands, they used them as bonding for their own hastily constructed walls. There is one large mass of overturned masonry close to the sea which illustrates this bonding very clearly. An even more striking instance is found south of the fortress. Here four pillars can be seen projecting horizontally from the sea-wall near to the

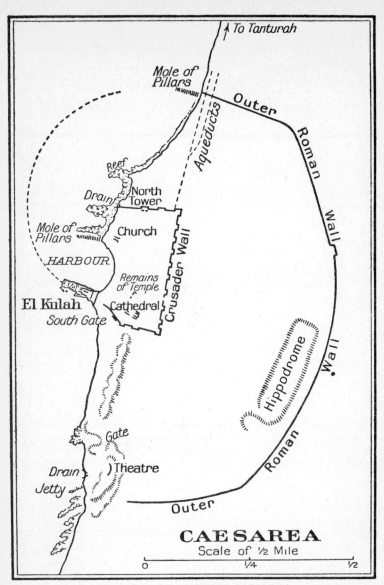

To Tanturah

Mole of Pillars

Aqueducts

Outer Roman Wall

Reef

Drain

North Tower

Mole of Pillars

Church

Crusader Wall

HARBOUR

Remains of Temple

El Kulah

Cathedral

South Gate

Hippodrome

Wall

Gate

Theatre

Drain

Jetty

Roman

Outer

CAESAREA

Scale of ½ Mile

0   ¼   ½

DIAGRAM OF ANCIENT CAESAREA

based upon Kitchener and Conder's Survey, corrected by modern aerial photographs. The dotted line, which is purely conjectural, indicates the possible course of Herod's mole, see full discussion on pp. 72–78

13. THE HARBOUR AT CAESAREA

A striking photograph obtained shortly before sunset

14. THE CITADEL AND REEF

Seen from a point close to the mole of pillars to the north of Caesarea Bay

Citadel, due possibly to the erosion of the sandstone in which they were originally set.

Indeed, so numerous were these pillars that the Crusaders also used them to construct an artificial reef or mole in the centre of the bay. Apparently the medieval navigators found the present harbour too shallow for the convenient unloading of their ships and they threw out this roughly improvised jetty for a distance of about two hundred feet. A striking photograph of the Crusaders' mole, taken in the late afternoon against the setting sun, is reproduced in Plate 17.

The most arresting visible feature of present-day Caesarea, however, is the medieval *donjon* or Citadel, *El Kulah*, which stands upon the base of the great natural reef to the south of the harbour. In some lights it makes a very impressive picture. The castle itself, once a massive structure, now very much decayed, was the key to the Crusader town on its seaward side. The Arabic historian, Al-Makrīzī, tells us that it was one of the strongest fortresses in Syria and that when Bibars attacked the town in A.D. 1265 "the people took refuge in the Citadel".

There is a cavity leading to the substructure which the villagers point out as the possible site of the prison of St. Paul. This identification is almost certainly mistaken. There is a far more ancient tradition which locates this prison in a crypt still preserved beneath the ruins of the Cathedral, which lie thirty or forty yards to the east of the reef.

We spent a good deal of time studying what remains

of this venerable church, which originally consisted of a nave and two aisles, terminating in three apses. Conder, who explored the site very thoroughly in 1878, noted that the building was about 28 degrees out of the east and west line—a fact not without significance, since the church was plainly erected upon ground originally occupied by the great Herodian Temple to Rome and Augustus.

Unfortunately the cathedral foundations have now been extensively built over by the Arabs, but the three apses of the original structure can still be distinguished. The small rectangular block of white stone shown in the foreground marks the grave of a former Superior of the Greek convent (Plate 18).

A sad story attaches to the modest dwelling reproduced on the extreme left of the photograph. This is the Greek monastery and at the time of our visit was presided over by Father Hanna El Khoury, a comparatively young priest of about thirty-five years of age. He rendered valuable service to our party and took a deep interest in our investigations. Late one night a few weeks after we left, the house was surrounded by revolutionaries, and the Greek monk and his brother were carried off forcibly to the hills. Their many friends feared the worst and presently the news filtered into Caesarea that the two men, who were much loved by the tiny community, had been shot. It was said that this was a reprisal for their having fired in self-defence upon their assailants.

Another interesting photograph of the Cathedral Com-

15. OVERTURNED MASONRY
on the shore at Caesarea showing sections of ancient pillars used as bonding
for the Crusader walls

16. PROJECTING PILLARS IN SEA WALL
near to the ruins of the Citadel at Caesarea

17. THE CRUSADER MOLE AT CAESAREA
Showing the use made of Herodian pillars to facilitate landing

plex, taken from the south-western or seaward side, shows the modern entrance to the "prison".

The Crusader walls, complete with glacis and moat, are still in places very well preserved, particularly on the northern side and the compact layout of the modern village is largely due to their survival and the protection they afford. Seen from the air this tiny mosaic of flat-roofed dwellings, marvellously preserving the medieval outline amid the surrounding wastes of sand, is one of the most arresting features of the landscape.

It is interesting to observe that there is an *open space* in present-day Caesarea which does not appear to have been built upon in ancient times. It lies between the Cathedral and the Citadel. Looking across this gap towards the sea I could not help speculating whether the hiatus may not indeed perpetuate the site of the atrium or courtyard of Herod's palace. If so, we were very near just then to one of the most significant incidents of Pilate's career.

2. ANCIENT CAESAREA

Outside the walls of this rather cramped medieval fortress—and in a sense dwarfing them completely—lie the remains of the much greater metropolis which Pilate knew. The vast circuit of the ancient ramparts, still plainly visible where they come down to the shore, testify to the scale upon which Herod the Great laid out this noble city, which had a frontage to the sea of over one mile.

In the centre of the long coastline, protected from the

south by the broad reef upon which *El Kulah* stands, lies a tiny bay which in turn is flanked by two lesser reefs running out into comparatively shallow water. The whole roadstead, as the map will show, is well within the compass of the Crusader fortifications.

Now here lies a very great mystery, because the historian, Josephus, who is our only authority for the original plan of the seaport and was, of course, contemporary with its most brilliant period, describes a harbour *so spacious that he does not hesitate to compare it with the Piraeus*[1] *at Athens.*

Quite frankly, it is impossible to reconcile this claim with the limited facilities provided by the present harbour. Indeed, more than one modern traveller coming to this modest bay—certainly no larger than many an obscure Cornish cove—has gone away with the conviction that Josephus was either romancing or has grossly exaggerated the facts. Even Conder, who surveyed the coast very thoroughly in 1878 seems to have thought that Herod's mole did not extend beyond the existing reef.

Having studied the problem with some care I am of opinion that this view is mistaken. It is well known that the harbour at Caesarea had an established reputation throughout the Graeco-Roman world as a commodious and safe anchorage. It was referred to as *Limen*

[1] There were three harbours in the Piraeus at Athens: Carinthus, Munychia and Zea. The former was by far the largest and is reputed to have accommodated 400 ships. It is probably this haven to which Josephus refers.

Sebastos and at one period its fame eclipsed that of the town itself. A coin of the time of Nero distinguishes the latter as "the Caesarea beside the August harbour". This wide repute could only have been acquired by the direct report of seafaring men who, by reason of their profession, would be familiar with the other great harbours of the Orient. The suggestion that it rested on nothing more than the facilities provided by the existing bay—exposed on its seaward side to all the fury of the elements—is plainly inadmissible.

It must not be forgotten, also, that the description of the seaport given by Josephus in the *Jewish War* was repeated by him almost verbatim in the *Antiquities*, written at a time when he was prosperously settled in Rome and had a reputation to preserve. This double publication suggests that he had nothing to fear from comparison with the city itself, which at that time was at the height of its glory.

Finally the historian gives a number of specific details concerning the harbour and the disposition of the shipping which are perfectly compatible with the construction which he describes but which are quite meaningless in relation to the existing bay.

So impressed was I by the force of these considerations that, at my special request, the British Air Ministry in London instructed one of the Haifa squadrons to take two aerial photographs of modern Caesarea from a height of about 400 feet. One of these (of the kind known as "vertical") shows the layout of the village with great clearness. The other is an "oblique" picture and brings out plainly the indented character of the coast north of the bay. (See Plates 20 and 21).

Now, Josephus tells us that Herod the Great built Caesarea upon the site of an obscure seaside place called Strato's Tower and that its construction occupied twelve years. He lays some stress on the fact that the coast at this point was not really suitable for an undertaking of this kind and speaks, rather significantly, of the "recalcitrant nature" of the site.

He claims, however, that by "dint of expenditure and enterprise the King triumphed over nature" and constructed a harbour which not only challenged its great rival at Athens but included "other deep roadsteads within its recesses". He then gives us the following detailed description of the port:

Having determined upon the comparative size of the harbour [i.e. larger than the Piraeus] [Herod] had blocks of stone let down into twenty fathoms of water, most of them measuring fifty feet in length by nine in depth and ten in breadth, some being even larger. Upon the submarine foundation thus laid he constructed above the surface a mole two hundred feet broad; of which one hundred were built out to break the surge, whence this portion was called the breakwater, while the remainder supported a stone wall encircling the harbour. From this wall arose, at intervals, massive towers, the loftiest and most magnificent of which was called Drusion after the step-son of Caesar.

Numerous inlets in the wall provided landing-places for mariners putting in to harbour, while the whole circular terrace fronting these channels served as a broad promenade

74

18. CATHEDRAL REMAINS AT CAESAREA

The three apses of the original building are shown in the foreground. The rectangular white stone marks the grave of a former Superior of the Greek Convent

19. PART OF THE CATHEDRAL COMPLEX

The doorway in the centre of the picture marks the entrance to the "Prison of St. Paul" for disembarking passengers. The entrance to the port faced northwards, because in these latitudes the north wind is the most favourable of all. At the harbour-mouth stood colossal statues, three on either side, resting on columns; the columns on the left of vessels entering port were supported by a massive tower, those on the right by two upright blocks of stone clamped together, whose height exceeded that of the tower on the opposite side. Abutting on the harbour were houses, also of white stone, and upon it converged the streets of the town, laid at equal distances apart. On an eminence facing the harbour-mouth stood Caesar's temple, remarkable for its beauty and grand proportions; it contained a colossal statue of the emperor, not inferior to the Olympian Zeus, which served for its model, and another of Rome, rivalling that of Hera at Argos. The city Herod dedicated to the province, the harbour to navigators in these waters, to Caesar the glory of this new foundation, to which he accordingly gave the name of Caesarea. (*Jewish War*, 1, 21, 6-7.)

Josephus also mentions the interesting fact that "towards the city [i.e. seen from the mole] there was a double station for the ships" and he speaks of a rather curious system of subterranean vaults and channels beneath the city:

Some of these vaults carried things at even distances to the haven and to the sea; but one of them ran obliquely, and bound all the rest together, that both the rain and the filth of the citizens were together carried off with ease, and the sea itself, upon the flux of the tide from without, came into the city, and washed it all clean. (*Antiquities*, 9, 6.)

Finally he tells us that:

Herod also built a theatre of stone; and on the south

quarter, behind the port, an amphitheatre capable of holding a vast number of men, and conveniently situated for a prospect to the sea. (*Antiquities*, 9, 6.)

All this reads like—and almost certainly is—the work of an eye-witness, a man who had actually landed upon the mole and seen the harbour crowded with shipping with the great Caesarean temples and palaces rising majestically behind. There are, however, four statements in this very vivid series of word-pictures, the significance of which is frequently overlooked, but which the modern student must take into account:

In the first place Josephus clearly implies that the mole was *circular* in form. He speaks of the "whole circular terrace fronting the landing places" and of the inner wall of the breakwater "encircling the harbour". He declares quite emphatically that the entrance to the port was on the *north*. He describes the haven as providing a *double station* for the ships. Lastly he speaks of other deep roadsteads within the *recesses* of the harbour.

To any one who studies attentively the photographic evidence adduced in these pages it will be clear that not a single one of these four vital conditions can be satisfied by any plausible reconstruction of the existing bay.

Let us assume (as is so frequently done) that all Herod did was to reinforce with a few giant stones the great natural reef upon which the Crusader Citadel, El Kulah, now stands. Precisely what protection did he secure for his shipping? Clearly very little, since the mouth of the bay would still be open to the fury of the elements. The

20. VERTICAL PHOTOGRAPH OF CAESAREA

Official Royal Air Force photograph. Note the marked northward
inclination of the great reef

21. CAESAREA FROM THE AIR

Official Royal Air Force photograph, specially taken at the author's suggestion to show
indentations of the coast north of the present harbour

entrance to this harbour would plainly be in the west. And what becomes of those curious references to a "double station" for the ships and to "*other* deep road-steads within the recesses of the harbour"?

I submit that the only intelligible way of fitting the description to the facts is to take Josephus roughly at his word and project the great reef in the form of a curved artificial mole into comparatively deep water. Only in this way could a riding station be provided for any considerable number of ships since, towards the shore, the bay is very shallow and even the Crusaders' jetty projects visibly for 200 feet.

I have indicated a possible line for Herod's mole upon the plan (see page 68). It is, of course, purely conjectural, but it satisfies two of our conditions. The landing-place is *circular* and the entrance to the port is on the north.

Curiously enough, when we take this rather bold step, we stumble almost unexpectedly upon a possible solution to our other difficulties. I suppose that no one who has personally visited Caesarea can fail to have observed the danger and inconvenience of the *two lesser reefs* which project into the sea slightly to the north of the Crusaders' mole. Their presence is plainly indicated by the flecks of foam in the aerial photographs but their formation is best studied in the plan.

In the nature of things these very treacherous reefs must always have been a characteristic feature of the site and in the absence of a true breakwater they would be a source of incessant peril to any shipping anchored near them. Certainly they could not have been overlooked by Herod's engineers and they are probably among the "recalcitrant features" referred to by Josephus.

It will be noted, however, that these reefs have deeper water on both sides and in the much ampler protected haven which we are now considering they would have the effect of dividing the harbour into *two parts*. We seem, therefore, to have a reasonable and consistent explanation of the statement of Josephus that there was a "double station" for the ships. This clustering of vessels into two clearly defined groups would be an outstanding impression in the mind of any visitor coming freshly to the port.

It is significant, too, that apart from the pronounced gap between the reefs referred to, the coast to the north of the Crusader town is much more highly indented than it is generally represented to be (see Plate 21), and it may be that we have here an explanation of the "other" deep roadsteads within the "recesses" of the harbour. Traces of a sea-wall can, in fact, be seen far to the north of the Crusader village.

Looking at these facts squarely, with the wind whistling through the ruins and the tempestuous sea breaking into foam on the rocks at our very feet, I came to the conclusion that it was more logical to accept the Josephan account of the general characteristics of the port than to adopt the alternative and critical view. Indeed, from a purely nautical standpoint, that alternative is practically meaningless.

This conviction was very greatly strengthened when, later in the day, we went down across the sand-hills to the southernmost point of the Roman city.

Here there are unmistakable traces of the Stone Theatre described by Josephus. This vast open-air theatre, directly facing the sea, was capable of seating several thousand spectators, and at some later period was apparently converted into a fortress. It is semi-circular in shape and the masonry is built deep into the side of a small hill upon which a rising tier of seats is still visible.

As though to emphasize the substantial accuracy of the Jewish historian, we found quite close to the theatre a great rectangular opening which is almost certainly part of the *drainage system* of ancient Caesarea by which, according to Josephus, "the sea itself, upon the flux of the tide from without, came into the city". I have included one photograph showing a local villager peering into the opening of this subterranean channel.

But perhaps the most impressive testimony to the credibility of Josephus lies in the vast Hippodrome to the south-east of the town, now completely overgrown with weeds and snake-ridden grass. It is comparable in size to the Circus Maximus at Rome and must have witnessed many costly displays under Herod and the Roman Procurators.

As we stood there in the late afternoon—the sound of the distant waves alone breaking the stillness—it seemed to us as though that vast amphitheatre had suddenly been projected backwards for two thousand years. The weeds had vanished and the encircling mound was white with thousands of excited men, shouting and cheering as the contending chariots raced swiftly round the arena, or as some favourite gladiator, engaged in a tense struggle to the death, gave the fatal thrust which proclaimed him victor.

We stumbled through the rank growth and came to a mighty granite pylon, now overthrown and lying on its side. Attempts have clearly been made to cut it into millstones. The stone, however, is of exceptional hardness and the project was abandoned. Two abortive incisions, several inches deep, are clearly shown in the picture.

In the centre of the great arena lay another stone of more than usual interest. It was broken into three pieces. The measure of that stone was thirty-seven and a half feet long, cut in one solid piece from some unknown quarry. How it came there, or what purpose it served, no one can say, but it is impressive to recall that it was just such titanic blocks as this which, according to Josephus, Herod the King let down into the Caesarean bay.

Later we visited the northern extremity of the Roman town where we found the aqueducts (first described by Kitchener and Conder in their famous survey of 1878) still marvellously preserved. The Low-Level Aqueduct brought water from the Zerka River and had a total length of about three miles. The High-Level Aqueduct relied chiefly upon springs in the neighbourhood of

22. OPEN SPACE AT CAESAREA

Lying between the Cathedral ruins and the Citadel

23. REMAINS OF STONE THEATRE

facing the sea to the south of the harbour at Caesarea

Subbarin, about eight miles distant, and crossed the
Zerka by a low bridge. These aqueducts, which are
undoubtedly of Roman origin, bear a striking resemblance to those which brought water from the "Pools of
Solomon" to the Temple in Jerusalem, a subject which
will be discussed fully in a later chapter.

The sun was already low down in the western sky
when we reharnessed our horses for the long trek across
the sandy wastes to Binyamina, where Lusho Fath'ullah,
tired out by his lonely vigil, had fallen asleep in the car.

Jerusalem was over one hundred kilometres distant.
We should be lucky if we reached the "King David"
before midnight. Fortunately the roads were comparatively clear, and as we sped along through the darkness
—our headlights weaving fantastic patterns upon the
cactus hedges and the deep silent groves—we fell to
talking of those far-off days when Caesarea stood in all
her pagan glory upon that desolate shore.

You must think of us engaged in animated conversation as our little car bumped her way over the rough
patches from Binyamina to Jaffa. Lusho was at the
wheel; my wife—her imagination fired by her experience
—in her chosen place of honour by the driver's side.
Goodwin and I occupied the rear seats.

Vividly the picture grew as each member of the little
party contributed some point of interest. Then when
Tel-Aviv was safely passed and we were fairly set on the
long straight run to the Judean heights, I tried to retell

to my companions the strange story of Pilate and the Roman Ensigns. It is a story of more than usual interest and before it was finished we had passed Kolonieh and the blue lights of Jerusalem were already glowing upon the eternal hills.

CHAPTER VI

PILATE FIRES THE FIRST SHOT

Now when the curtain first rises upon the drama of that stormy decade the little ship which we left ploughing the Sicilian seas has come safely into port and Pilate is installed in the Herodian Palace at Caesarea. The year is A.D. 26, and the Procurator is already in trouble with his new subjects.

Josephus describes the incident at some length in his *Jewish War* and the reader may find it convenient to have the full text before him. I give it below in William Whiston's well-known English translation:

> Now Pilate, who was sent as a procurator into Judea by Tiberius, sent by night those images of Caesar that are called *ensigns* into Jerusalem. This excited a very great tumult among the Jews when it was day; for those who were near them were astonished at the sight of them, as indications that their laws were trodden under foot; for those laws do not permit any sort of image to be brought into the city. Nay, besides the indignation which the citizens had themselves at this procedure, a vast number of people came running out of the country. These came zealously to Pilate to Caesarea, and besought him to carry those ensigns out of Jerusalem, and to preserve them their ancient laws inviolable; but upon

Pilate's denial of their request, they fell down prostrate upon the ground, and continued immovable in that posture for five days and as many nights.

On the next day Pilate sat upon his tribunal, in the open market place, and called to him the multitude, as desirous to give them an answer; and then gave a signal to the soldiers that they should all by agreement at once encompass the Jews with their weapons; so the band of soldiers stood round about the Jews in three ranks. The Jews were under the utmost consternation at that unexpected sight. Pilate also said to them that they should be cut in pieces unless they would admit of Caesar's images, and gave intimation to the soldiers to draw their naked swords. Hereupon the Jews, as it were at one signal, fell down in vast numbers together, and exposed their necks bare, and cried out that they were sooner ready to be slain than that their laws should be transgressed. Hereupon Pilate was greatly surprised at their prodigious superstition, and gave order that the ensigns should be presently carried out of Jerusalem.

Such is the earliest account of this famous incident which has descended to us. About eighteen years later, however, Josephus retold the story and in this study, written after mature reflection, he adds some touches which are not only interesting in themselves but contribute to a clearer understanding of what happened.

He tells us, for example, that the occasion for the Jewish protest was given by the removal of the army from Caesarea to Jerusalem "*to take up their winter quarters in that city*". He confirms that the actual entry into the capital "*was done in the night time*", and he adds the interesting statement that former Procurators were wont to make their entry with ensigns which did not carry the

24. THE ROMAN HIPPODROME

Now choked with weeds and long grass. Note the massive granite pylon with incisions

25. IN THE HIPPODROME AT CAESAREA

Pieces of a broken block of stone measuring 37 feet in length. Probably from the same quarry as that used by Herod to reinforce the sea-mole

offending effigies. *"Pilate was the first who brought those images to Jerusalem"*. Finally, instead of representing the Governor as being surprised at the prodigious superstition of the people, he describes him as being "deeply affected with their firm resolution to keep their laws inviolate, and presently commanded the images to be carried back from Jerusalem to Caesarea."

All this, of course, is in very marked contrast to Philo's sweeping and angry denunciation of Pilate's character. According to Josephus, the incident passed off entirely without bloodshed. No one, apparently, was penalized for organizing a movement which might, quite plausibly, have been regarded as a personal affront to Caesar. The Jews, moreover, clearly gained their point and the Procurator took appropriate steps to remedy the grievance. If all Pilate's affairs were of this relatively mild character, there would be little to justify the Alexandrian's charge of "never-ending and grievous inhumanity".

A closer study of the combined narratives, however, brings out certain points which are of great interest. In the first place we are able to date the incident, with almost complete certainty, as taking place in the autumn of A.D. 26. Pilate arrived at Caesarea about the middle of the year and the sending of the "army" to "take up its winter quarters" in the capital was plainly the prelude to his first visit to Jerusalem. Had a State entry previously been made into the city with the offending ensigns, the trouble would assuredly have arisen earlier.

It is quite certain, also, that the act was deliberate, and

that Pilate was fully conscious of its significance. Personally I can see no reason to doubt the assertion of Josephus that it was the practice of the earlier Procurators to avoid offending the Jewish susceptibilities by sending standards which did not bear the actual effigy of Caesar. It was one of those small concessions to Oriental prejudice which a great Colonial Power like Rome could readily afford to make and, generally speaking, it was part of her genius to do so. Pilate must have known of this practice. The fact that he sent in the military contingents *by night*—a very unusual time for such manœuvres—shows that he suspected that it might lead to trouble.

Finally, the reader will observe that Josephus makes no reference whatever to any organized or official protest from Jerusalem. The mob which swarmed into Caesarea and clamoured for five days at the gates of the Herodian Palace consisted (according to our author) of "indignant citizens" and a "vast number of people which came running out of the country". *Neither Annas nor Caiaphas, nor any recognized member of the ruling caste in Jerusalem appears in the story.*

Now why was that?

It may be, of course, that the zeal of the people outran the slow-moving and rather cumbrous machinery of the Jewish State. Rumour travels very quickly in a small country like Palestine and the first waves of the popular protest against the introduction of the ensigns may easily have reached Caesarea before a formal delegation could be instructed and sent upon its way. This would account for the spontaneous and apparently unorganized character of the demonstration recorded by Josephus and, incidentally, make Pilate's reversal of his original order much easier.

But the lapse of five days without any visible sign of official intervention is significant. It suggests that at this very critical juncture, Joseph Caiaphas—one of the subtlest brains in Syria and the real dictator of Jewry at this period—was biding his time.

For some weeks this priestly autocrat, sitting in his rich apartments in the best quarter of Jerusalem, must have been wondering—a little anxiously—what sort of a man the new Procurator, Pontius Pilate, might prove to be. His anxiety was justified. Four times in eleven years had Valerius Gratus, the retiring Governor, deposed the High Priest and installed another in his place. Caiaphas happened to be the latest nominee, but would his luck hold with a new Procurator reported to be in high favour, not only with the Emperor, but with that arch-hater of the Jews, Sejanus himself? It was a dangerous moment for Caiaphas when Pilate landed, after his long journey, upon the quay at Caesarea.

Then came the bombshell.

Suddenly and without warning Pilate fired the first shot and there could be no uncertainty about its meaning. In the early hours of a September morning some one must have burst into the private apartments of Caiaphas with the disquieting message: "The Romans came in during the night. . . . They have brought in the forbidden ensigns. . . . Already there is uproar in the city."

This sudden and dramatic move on the part of the new Procurator was, to say the least, highly inconvenient. Caiaphas had many reasons for desiring his first meeting with Pilate to be as noncommittal as possible. It would give him time to take the measure of his new master and to exert his influence in favour of the *status quo*. The prosperity of Caiaphas—the very foundations of his great fortune—rested upon a *concordat* with Rome. And here he was, committed at the outset to an angry disputation in which he must perforce take, not the Roman, but the Jewish side. If ever a subtle and scheming dictator was placed upon the horns of a dilemma it was Caiaphas on that fateful morning.

The adroit Sadducean seems, however, to have turned the situation very deftly to his own advantage. There can be little doubt that a meeting of the Sanhedrin was summoned, since so grave a violation of the Mosaic Law challenged the highest and most sacred principle of the Jewish State. Caiaphas must have listened to some extremely plain speaking, but in his official capacity as Acting High Priest and ex-officio leader of the Assembly, it was at once his duty and his interest to counsel moderation.

We can picture him sitting in his place in the centre of the Assembly listening with some embarrassment, but outwardly with unruffled calm, to the debate. Then in a few cold sentences he would put the hard, unalterable facts.

There was nothing to be gained by an immediate and sanguinary clash with the now augmented garrison in the fortress of Antonia. The ensigns could only be recalled by the direct order of the Governor and he was sixty miles away at Caesarea. Better to wait and settle with him personally than to risk the utter subjugation of the Jewish State. Moreover, report said that the provincials were already rising in protest. Pilate would hear of this quickly enough. If any one was to take a false step at this critical juncture let the Procurator himself do it.

Such were the sort of arguments with which an astute and resourceful leader could counsel and ensure delay. There would, of course, be malcontents. Many hot and futile words would be spoken, but in the end the security of the State was paramount. On a show of hands Caiaphas would probably get his way.

Consider now the reverse side of the shield.

We must think of Pilate arriving at Caesarea after his long journey. As the little ship came slowly to her moorings in the great harbour, he must have seen the white Temple of Augustus and the magnificent Herodian Palace, his future residence, reflected in the waters and felt something of the thrill which comes to every man starting upon a new and decisive phase of his career. Here was the Province in which for the next few years he would hold undisputed sway and from which he hoped to extract the nucleus of his future fortune.

The vast city, with its spacious harbour, and its fine

buildings must have seemed very familiar to the Procurator, and inspired him with a consciousness of the dignity of his new office. Here, at least, was a bit of Rome. Judea, the land of seething discontent, of stormy passions, of ceaseless pilgrimages to the Fortress-Temple of Jerusalem, lay beyond. He would explore that presently. For the moment there was work enough in settling down to the normal routine of government.

Slowly and imperceptibly, however, Jerusalem would make her distant presence felt. Many of the problems affecting Roman law and property; disputes between Greeks, Samaritans and Jews; the upkeep and repair of buildings, and the maintenance of public order, would come from the capital. There were documents to read and sign, accounts of public dues to receive and ratify; provisional decisions to endorse; sentences, in the case of delayed judgments, to be ratified; in short, all the dull but necessary tasks in the life of a high official of the State. Sooner or later, too, the vital question of confirming (or otherwise) the semi-political appointment of the High Priest would come up for review. The Romans could brook no disloyalty in the occupant of the supreme office of the Jewish State.

In this matter Pilate would doubtless be influenced by the experience of the retiring Governor who had put Caiaphas in office. If the two men did meet in Alexandria, Valerius Gratus, rendered cynical by eleven years' contact with one of the most turbulent and difficult peoples in the Orient, probably expressed himself very vigorously with regard to the wealthy Sadducean families which at this period dominated Jerusalem.

We can imagine him taking Pilate aside and saying in effect: "You will find those fellows a very tricky lot. I had to depose four of them before I could get my way. From your point of view Caiaphas is probably the safest. He professes to mean well towards Rome and you can trust him up to a point. But he will be quick to discern weakness and turn it to his own advantage. If you decide to keep him—and you might do worse—ride him with a tight rein."

So, as the time came for his first official visit to the capital, we find Pilate taking a step which to his brusque and objective type of mind doubtless seemed an astute stroke of statesmanship. *He would let the High Priest know that he was not the man to stand any nonsense.* His subsequent dealings with Caiaphas would be rendered all the easier by his having scored the first point.

In choosing these particular ensigns, however, as the symbol of his authority, Pilate made one of the biggest miscalculations of his life. The blow aimed at the priest-hood recoiled upon him from a direction whence he least expected it.

Within a few hours of the arrival of the Roman garri-son, rumour had carried the news of the outrage to the surrounding villages. Swiftly the popular ferment grew and, before the astonished Procurator realized the full consequences of his act, a steadily growing crowd of excited Hebrews had begun to gather outside his palace in Caesarea.

It is to the credit of Pilate that he endured this angry eruption of a fanatical populace for five days without taking measures to disperse the crowds. Most probably they were days of anxious conference with his advisers. We can imagine Claudia standing at one of the windows of the palace and looking down upon the clamour below, fearing for her husband's future. No Procurator within living memory had aroused so formidable a demonstration within a few weeks of taking office. The symptoms were disquieting. If this could happen in Caesarea, what sort of a fire was smouldering in Jerusalem itself?

Pontius Pilate, compelled at last to face the crowd in person, seems to have decided to play the ancient game of bluff. He made as though he was going to consider their request and had a seat carried to the open space facing the palace, concealing nearby a detachment of soldiers. When the clamour began again he caused the demonstrators to be surrounded and threatened them with instant death if they did not cease troubling him.

It was the sort of manœuvre which was usually successful in the case of disorder among subject peoples, but this particular demonstration was not of that kind. Here was no organized rebellion against the power and might of Rome. The opposition sprang solely from the outraged feelings of the common people, and Pilate had the sense to recognize it for what it was.

26. THE "HOUSE OF CAIAPHAS"
Showing approach to the present building on the South West Hill

27. THE "HOUSE OF CAIAPHAS"
Showing interior view of the building

When the leaders, confronted by this terrible alternative, bared their necks to the executioner's sword, Pilate's last argument had gone. A rebellious mob he would probably have dispatched without mercy. He could not murder in cold blood a submissive people. Imperial Rome had her own standards of chivalry and religious toleration.

Ultimately the new Procurator took the only sensible course. He gave his word that the ensigns would be removed and kept it. The crowds dispersed to their homes. Next day there was jubilation throughout all Judea. . . .

Such, briefly, is the story of the Caesarean episode as I tried to describe it to my companions during that memorable night ride from Binyamina to Jerusalem.

Suddenly Lusho Fath'ullah applied the brakes and Goodwin stepped out. The tall, white tower of the Y.M.C.A. building shimmered in the moonlight, seeming to pierce the deep blue of the Judean sky. We were at the gates of the King David Hotel. With many fervent thanks to our friends for a safe escort, we said "Good night" and retired to bed.

The air in the room was close, and I went out on to the verandah, glad of the cool breeze which was blowing across the heights. Jerusalem was very quiet, her inhabitants sunk in slumber, but the brilliant arc lamps on the Bethlehem Road threw a lovely radiance upon the grey solid wall of the inner city. For the hundredth time my eye sought the dark spot on the crenellated wall beside which stands the so-called House of Caiaphas.

The clock seemed to go backwards to those remote days when Pilate had yet to enter that forbidding fortress, and as I stood there in the darkness with the ageless city at my feet, I knew that already the drama was quickening into a clash of wills, a duel between two men for the political soul of Jewry.

And the significant thing is that in the opening phase of that duel the cooler and more calculating brain triumphed. Caiaphas had undoubtedly won the first round.

CHAPTER VII

BACK TO JERUSALEM

We have now seen Pilate in action during the early, critical weeks of his official career—the period during which he was feeling, as it were, for the "controls" of the administrative machine through which for ten long years he was to guide the destinies of Judea. The impression which we receive is that of a rather aggressive type of military officer, very conscious of his status as Governor of a province, but lacking that deeper insight into the Oriental character which, perhaps, only a prolonged sojourn in the East could give.

We must regard him provisionally, I think, as a rather impulsive man, apt to form his decisions swiftly without taking full count of the remoter consequences of his acts. He is like a chess-player, confronted by an unfamiliar gambit and strongly tempted to make the spectacular rather than the sound and cautious move. Moreover, he is a little impatient of tradition, dismissing the more conciliatory moods of his predecessors as a sign of weakness—derogatory alike to his own personal prestige and to the sovereignty of Rome. These are clear inferences from the statement of Josephus that Pilate was the first of the Procurators to send the hated *imperatorum imagines* into the city.[1]

In strict fairness, however, we must admit that there was really very little in this episode to justify the invective of Philo or to support the more serious charges which he brings against Pilate. Without doubt the new Governor committed a grave political blunder in sending the forbidden ensigns into Jerusalem. For that dangerous and highly provocative act there is no semblance of excuse. The traditional practice in this matter must have been perfectly well known to even the humblest member of the Roman guard and a more cautious administrator would have respected that tradition.

But, having made the blunder and observed its effect, Pilate at least rectified the mistake in a way which met the Jewish objection in full. The images were withdrawn and the incident seems to have closed on terms which left no permanent cause for resentment or ill-will.

The problem which now confronts us, therefore, is to ascertain whether this cross-section of the Procurator's character is true to type, and immediately upon my return from Caesarea I began to make plans for what I knew would prove to be a very arduous and difficult inquiry. It concerned the *water supply* of Jerusalem in ancient

[1] It is interesting to note that, according to the Roman historian, Tacitus, the Gauls also disliked these effigies of Caesar. "The images of the Emperors were torn down from the ensigns; and the Roman standards, stripped of their ornaments, seemed to droop in disgrace, while the colours of the Gauls fluttered in the air and glittered to the eye."—Tacitus, *Hist.*, 4, 52.

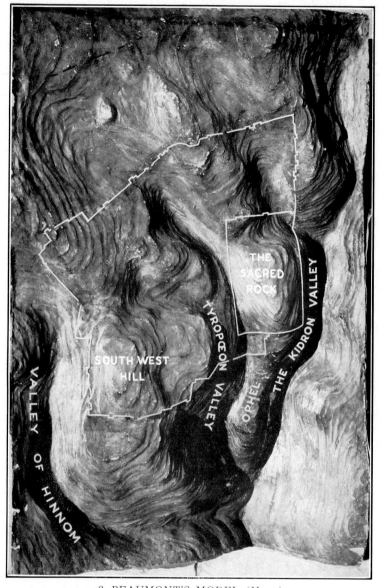

28. BEAUMONT'S MODEL (No. 1)
Specially designed to show the original depth and contour of the valleys
around Jerusalem

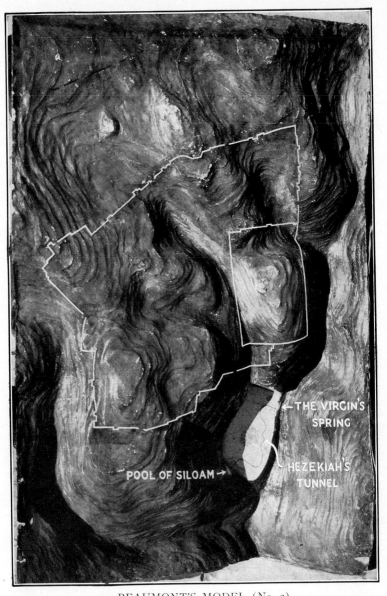

THE VIRGIN'S SPRING

POOL OF SILOAM →

HEZEKIAH'S TUNNEL

29. BEAUMONT'S MODEL (No. 2)

In this photograph the hill "Ophel" has been removed, revealing the famous rock tunnel connecting the Virgin's Spring with the Pool of Siloam

times and particularly during the period of the Roman Procurators. I was fortunate in securing the assistance and advice of a number of distinguished scholars residing in the district. Without their profound knowledge of the results of recent excavation and of the conflicting theories advanced to explain them, this book could never have been written. I am specially indebted to Mr. P. L. O. Guy, Director of the British School of Archaeology in Jerusalem; to Dr. Sukenik, of the Hebrew University; to the Staff of the Department of Antiquities; and to Mr. J. D. Whiting, of the American Colony, to whose careful studies of the aqueduct systems special reference will be made later.

It quickly became evident, however, that the investigation upon which I was engaged was unusual and in a certain sense unique. Apparently no one within living memory had gone to Palestine for the express and limited purpose which I had in mind, viz. to search for authentic relics of *Pontius Pilate*, and a great deal of the material had to be dug out, as it were, afresh from the vast mass of archaeological data which had accumulated over a period of about sixty years. Much of this was already out of date and had to be adjusted to the newer ideas, based upon more recent exploration, which have revitalized our study of the old city.

Fortunately the more important exhibits were still *in situ* and, when records were obscure or non-existent, the camera could be brought in to redress the balance. This was very effectively done by my friend, Mr. G. Eric

G

Matson—one of the ablest photographers of the Near East—for whose indefatigable efforts in this connection no praise can be too high. He risked his life more than once, during the recent disturbances, to obtain pictures in lonely and secluded places and the illustrations throughout this book are his work.

But why—the reader may ask—this peculiar pre-occupation with the question of *water*? Every great community in the past has been dependent upon an adequate supply of this vital necessity of life and has solved the problem in its own way. Jerusalem surely was no exception. Why should this apparently common-place and routine matter of civil administration assume such special significance in the case of Pontius Pilate?

I have already given a hint of the answer to this question in an earlier chapter, but the time has now come when we must face the problem boldly and in detail, because there *is* something peculiar about the ancient water systems of Jerusalem and it is vital to our interpretation of Pilate's story that the reader should understand what it is.

For this reason I shall try first to exhibit clearly the unique position of the ancient city in relation to the hills upon which it stood, and here we can use to advantage something which greatly aroused my interest during an early visit to the quiet and restful retreat of the American Colony.

We were having tea with our friends, Mr. and Mrs. Matson, and I was discussing with them the rather strange quest which had brought us to Jerusalem. The ladies of the party, finding these academic questions rather dull, ultimately drifted into animated conversation and, after the cups had been cleared away, Matson tapped me on the shoulder and said: "Come with me, I have something to show you."

He led the way to a broad corridor in which was set a trestle carrying a large-scale relief model of Jerusalem and its immediate surroundings, the work of Mr. E. F. Beaumont, formerly a member of the Colony.

The great interest of this model lies in the fact that it is very accurately designed to show the original depth and contour of the valleys before the long series of historic sieges had choked them with debris. When we had gazed at this in silence for some moments, Matson, rather unexpectedly, laid his hand upon the hill Ophel and *lifted it completely away.*

"I thought this would interest you!" he said.

Beneath the hill, clearly marked with all its strange windings, was the famous rock tunnel, cut by Hezekiah and his engineers to divert the water of the Virgin's Spring to the Pool of Siloam.

The story is partly told in the Second Book of Chronicles, Ch. 32, v. 2–4:

And when Hezekiah saw that Sennacherib was come, and that he was purposed to fight against Jerusalem, he took counsel with his princes and his mighty men to stop the waters of the fountains which were without the city; and they helped him. So there was gathered much people to-

99

gether, and they stopped all the fountains, and the brook which flowed through the midst of the land, saying: Why should the Kings of Assyria come and find much water?

We get a more explicit reference to this tunnel in II Kings, Ch. 20, v. 20, where we are told that Hezekiah "made the pool and the conduit and brought water into the city". The Chronicler confirms this by saying: "He sealed the issue of the waters of Gihon the upper and directed them down westwards to the city of David."

I felt that Mr. Beaumont's very ingenious model deserved a much wider publicity than it has yet received and the next morning we took two photographs under strong artificial illumination from the western side. The effects of light and shade thus produced are those normally manifested on the terrain itself shortly before sunset. For the convenience of the general reader I have indicated the outline of the existing city and the names of the principal valleys in white (see Plates 28 and 29).

Now the hill Ophel, which is so conspicuous a feature of these photographs, is of very profound archaeological interest. It was the original site of the ancient settlement which David captured from the Jebusites and it contains beneath its surface a number of subterranean workings which, in a sense, epitomize three supreme and critical phases in the history of Jerusalem.

We must try to project our minds backwards through the long dim vistas of the past to those primitive days when the Jebusites first established their little fortress on the top of this hill. Strategically it was well nigh impreg-

30. THE VIRGIN'S SPRING
From immemorial times one of the few sources of living water in the vicinity of Jerusalem

31. HEZEKIAH'S TUNNEL
Showing the exit at the Pool of Siloam

nable, since it was protected on three sides by deep valleys. Only on the north was it joined by an easily defensible ridge to the high ground upon which Aranauh had his threshing-floor and upon which Solomon ultimately built the first Temple.

From the Jebusites' point of view, the site was thus almost ideal and we can imagine them looking down from the security of their fortress upon the deep ravines below and boasting (as they did later) that "the blind and the lame" could defend that stronghold against the assaults of any likely enemy.

There was, however, as the modern saying goes, one rather serious "snag"—the age-old problem of water. There were no springs upon those stony and desolate heights and the ridge which joined them, as it were, to the mainland was too narrow and too close to the watershed to arrest more than a fraction of the rainfall.

Deep down, however, in the Kidron Valley, at the foot of the precipitous eastern slope of Ophel, was a cave from which gushed an intermittent but very copious spring, which overflowed its basin at regular intervals and sent water in a little rivulet along the base of the hill. Doubtless a path existed, as it does to-day, down the steep hillside to this famous spring and in times of peace the Jebusites could obtain all the water they needed. But let an enemy appear in the valley below and the defenders were immediately cut off from this vital and abundant source.

The perils attendant upon this situation must have

been realized at a very early date, because at some unknown period, using very primitive tools, the defenders of this ridge bored a subterranean channel down to the spring. They began by driving a tunnel from the existing cave for a distance of about fifty feet into the rock. They then sank a vertical shaft down to the level of the water, approached by a sloping gallery to which access was gained from a surface-opening within the fort. Thus, if the hill should be invested by an enemy, there was a secret and safe passage to the indispensable supplies of pure water.

Centuries later, when David challenged their supremacy, the Jebusites seem to have overlooked the dangers inherent in this secret approach to the heart of their citadel and many scholars believe that this subterranean passage was the very "shaft" (Hebrew *tsinnor*) by which Joab climbed up and surprised the garrison.[1]

So far as we know Joab's brilliant exploit was accomplished about the year 1040 B.C. and about three hundred years later there arose another crisis in the history of Jerusalem. By that time the so-called David's Burgh had spread northwards to embrace the Sacred Rock, over which towered the glittering fabric of Solomon's Temple. The city had also crossed the Tyropean Valley, climbing the terraced sides of the South-West Hill. The wall was now extended to include the summits of both hills

---

[1] For a full description of the great shaft, first discovered by Sir Charles Warren in 1867, and named after him, see Vincent's *Underground Jerusalem*, London, Horace Cox, 1911.

and to protect the lower reaches of the central valley.

Hezekiah was on the throne, and Sennacherib was already threatening to attack and subdue the city. Temporarily he was "bought off" by a tribute of gold, stripped from the doors and pillars of the Temple itself. But Hezekiah and his counsellors were not deceived by this respite. They knew that the wily Assyrian would come again, and in a few months of feverish activity they carried through a piece of engineering which will always remain one of the wonders of the ancient world.

The problem was to seal up the mouth of the cave and divert the waters of the spring inside the city. This could only be achieved by boring a tunnel *right through the hill*. They began at both ends (a mark of the urgency attached to its completion) and after many windings, due partly to their imperfect equipment, the working parties met midway. The point where the picks went through can still be discerned by those sufficiently interested to explore the tunnel.

Thus the precious waters of the Virgin's Spring first began to flow, as they do to-day, through the base of the mountain into the Upper Pool of Siloam. At long last the supply was secured exclusively for the inhabitants of Jerusalem. No longer could an enemy come to the foot of those steep cliffs and "find much water".

A closer inspection of the entrance to the Virgin's Cave shows that in ancient times no fewer than three attempts were made to carry the surplus water of the spring through rock-like channels along the *base of the hill*, but at a higher level than that of the torrent bed of the Kidron Valley. It is generally agreed that the purpose of these channels was to irrigate the King's Gardens and other cultivated spaces which are known to have existed at the junction of the valleys from early times.

From this brief description of the hill Ophel and the numerous workings associated with the Virgin's Spring, one fact emerges very clearly, viz. that from the earliest periods of her history the inhabitants of Jerusalem have been *very deeply concerned with the problem of water*.

The significance of this fact can hardly be over-stressed, because when the curtain next rises—upon the second act of this strange drama—the scene is set against a background of great aqueducts, bringing water from remote and mighty reservoirs into the very heart of the Holy City. And Pontius Pilate is once again the central figure in that stormy and tumultuous scene.

CHAPTER VIII

THE RIDDLE OF THE AQUEDUCTS

FORTUNATELY Josephus has left us two versions of the incident and in the earlier of these (the *Jewish War*) he tells the story thus:

> After this Pilate raised another disturbance, by expending that sacred treasure which is called Corban upon aqueducts, whereby he brought water from the distance of four hundred furlongs. At this the multitude had indignation: and when Pilate was come to Jerusalem, they came about his tribunal, and made a clamour at it. Now when he was apprised aforehand of this disturbance, he mixed his own soldiers in their armour with the multitude, and ordered them to conceal themselves under the habits of private men, and not indeed to use their swords, but with their staves to beat those who made the clamour. He then gave the signal from his tribunal. Now the Jews were so sadly beaten, that many of them perished as trodden to death by themselves; by which means the multitude was astonished at the calamity of those that were slain, and held their peace.

We may disregard for the moment the social and political consequences of Pilate's act—these will form the subject of a separate chapter—and concentrate our attention upon the original causes of the riot. These are clearly stated by Josephus in his opening sentence and there are three aspects of this statement which are of rather special interest.

First. The word "aqueducts" is in the *plural*. The significance of this point, which can hardly be accidental, will become clearer when we have examined the complex system of water channels in the neighbourhood of Solomon's Pools.

Second. The work was financed out of the *Sacred Treasury*, a fund which was specially ear-marked for religious purposes and which in normal circumstances could only be used by the direct authority of the High Priest.

Third. It is clearly implied in the narrative that the aqueducts were completed. The words of the historian are explicit. Pilate *expended* the money and *brought water* to the city.

Incidentally Josephus confirms the two last-mentioned points in the *Antiquities*, where he tells us that the Procurator "undertook to bring a current of water to Jerusalem and *did it* with the sacred money". In this later account, however, written when the historian was firmly established in Rome under Imperial patronage, he gives the distance as 200 instead of 400 stadia. Eusebius, who had both works before him, and was apparently puzzled by the discrepancy, quotes the *Antiquities'* passage but gives the length of the aqueduct as *300* stadia. The variant reading may, of course, have been in the copy of Josephus which Eusebius used, but it seems to me more probable that, in the interests of truth, he deliberately chose the mean between the two figures. Now the Greek "stade" was a standard measure of length roughly equal to 606 English feet. We have to look, therefore, for some artificial construction by which water was actually conducted over a distance varying from 23 to 46 miles! Remember that Jerusalem stood elevated upon her immemorial hills and since gravitation was normally employed for works of this kind, the source of the water must be substantially *higher* than its ultimate destination in the city itself.

These conditions can only be satisfied on the south side of Jerusalem, where the central range rises imperceptibly to the high ground around Hebron, and it is significant that along this line *the remains still exist of two very ancient aqueducts*. They both originate in the neighbourhood of three artificial reservoirs which are known to the Arabs as *El Burak* ("the pools") but which are more commonly referred to as the Pools of Solomon.

Clearly these Pools are a vital link in the investigation upon which we are now engaged, and in a later page I shall try to state plainly the conclusions which I personally reached with regard to them. These conclusions, of course, commit no one, but they are at least the result of an honest attempt to apply the principles of logic and common sense to an archaeological problem of profound interest.

Let us, therefore, in the first instance look at these mysterious Pools from the air. They lie about six and a half miles to the south-west of Jerusalem and in Plate 32 the reader will find a characteristic photograph, taken by Eric Matson, from a height of about 2,000 feet.

Seen from this rather unfamiliar angle the desolate character of the surroundings comes out very forcibly. The three reservoirs can be seen descending in steps to the wooded valley below. Across the picture (from left to right), reduced by the distance to a tiny white ribbon, runs the main road from Jerusalem to Hebron. Towards the centre a branch road, also rendered conspicuous by the glare of the Judean sun, unites the highroad with the Pools and the lower reaches of the Artas valley.

Seeing the Pools thus for the first time in distant perspective, the outstanding impression left upon my own mind was frankly one of amazement. I thought instinctively of the vast reservoirs at Lake Vyrnwy and the Elan Valley in Wales, designed to meet the needs of the dense industrial populations of Liverpool and Birmingham. Indeed there was an air of modernity about the whole installation which one associated more readily with recent rather than with ancient times.[1]

Yet so distinguished and keen an observer as the late Dr. Schick, who made an exhaustive study of the Pools as long ago as 1870, did not hesitate to attribute their original construction to Solomon! Others have assigned them to one of the later Kings of Judah or to the period of the Maccabees. Even Sir George Adam Smith, whose guesses have so often proved to be well founded, gave

1 This impression is not seriously affected by the fact that, after the Great War, the Jerusalem authorities reconditioned the masonry and established a pipe-line between the Pools and Jerusalem. I was fortunate in obtaining some excellent photographs of the reservoirs taken prior to this modern reconstruction. (See Frontispiece.)

32. THE "POOLS OF SOLOMON"

photographed from the air. Note the desolate character of the surroundings. The Jerusalem-
Hebron road is seen crossing the picture

33. THE "POOLS OF SOLOMON"

A closer view of the upper pool, showing the Saracenic Castle guarding the approach

it as his opinion that the lowest probable date was the reign of Herod the Great.

Here, then, is the first and, in one sense, the most pressing aspect of the riddle.

Thousands of years ago some far-seeing and competent mind came to the head of this fertile little valley and saw its possibilities. Four springs escaped from the living rock in its immediate vicinity.[1] The level was *eighty feet above the site of the Temple in Jerusalem.* The valley was therefore admirably suited for the purpose to which it has been put.

Who first conceived the daring plan of trapping the water of these springs and conducting it by great aqueducts to the Holy City? Did Solomon, the son of David, add to the triumphs which so impressed the Queen of Sheba this vast engineering work, or was it left to the restless and ambitious brain of Herod? Failing that, did Pontius Pilate perchance himself build the Pools and the aqueducts and thus "bring water" to the city?

These are questions of profound interest, to which tradition gives us no sure or certain reply. In the last resort we must rely upon our observations of the existing remains and try to interpret them in the light of reason and common sense.

[1] The four springs were these: (1) 'Ain Saleh, close to the present Hebron Road, known for the last three centuries as "the *sealed fountain*". This is connected by an underground channel with the Upper Pool. (2) 'Ain el-Burak, in the immediate vicinity of the present castle. (3) 'Ain Farujeh, which springs from a vault below the Lower Pool. (4) 'Ain 'Atan, on the slope to the south-west of the Pools. A fifth spring, 'Ain 'Artas, lies farther down the valley close to the village of that name. This, according to Dr. Schick, supplied the water for the Herodium aqueduct.

In order that we may visualize clearly the basic issues involved, I have asked my friend, Mr. Frederick Griffin —an artist with a happy gift for such subjects—to prepare a drawing of the Pools seen from an imaginary viewpoint about a hundred feet above the level of the Artas valley (see Plate 34). The square structure at the corner of the Upper Pool is of Saracenic origin and is known to the Arabs as Kalat-el-Burak (The Castle of the Pools). It is said to have been built as a means of protecting the reservoirs from the Bedouin. It is of no importance to our present inquiry, save that it occupies the site of one of the ancient springs and may have had its counterpart in Roman times.

We may therefore confine our attention for the moment to observing three broad general characteristics of the landscape.

(*a*) It will be noted that the reservoirs ascend the valley in a *series of steps*, so that the whole contents of the two upper pools can, if necessary, be drained off into the lower.

(*b*) Of the four ancient springs in the immediate vicinity only *two* are sufficiently high up *to deliver water to the Pools*. The 'Ain Farujeh escapes from a vault beneath the lowest pool, while the level of 'Ain 'Atan is also too low to affect the contents of the reservoir.

(*c*) The high ground upon which the castle stands continues as a ridge along the edge of the valley. Thus an aqueduct starting from this point in the direction of Jerusalem can *maintain its altitude* for a considerable distance.

With this panoramic view before us, we are now in a position to make a preliminary inspection of the aqueducts, and here I must warn the reader that he must begin to think, not in terms of a comparatively straightforward artificial channel, but of a vast network of waterways stretching for many miles on both sides of the Pools. Indeed, so far-reaching are the ramifications of this system that they can only be rendered effectively by means of three separate plans or diagrams.

For our general convenience we will call them Plans 1, 2 and 3, and reference should be made to them in that order.

Plan 1 is a map of Southern Judea showing the course taken by the so-called *High-Level* and *Low-Level aqueducts* designed to bring water from the Pools of Solomon to Jerusalem. It will be noted that this map shows a third aqueduct running from a point south of the Pools to the ancient ruins of Herodium, one of the massive fortresses built by Herod the Great. It will be observed also that the remains of the High-Level Aqueduct disappear abruptly about two miles south of the city. The Low-Level conduit can be traced the whole distance from the Pools to the great cisterns beneath the Temple area.

Plan 2 carries the story a stage further. It shows how the ancient engineers supplemented the normal resources of the Pools by tapping springs high up in the surrounding hills. Here again there are two aqueducts, named respectively from the valleys which they traverse: the Wady-el-Biar and the Wady 'Arrub.

Plan 3 shows the extraordinarily ingenious way in which the water from these aqueducts was made available, either to replenish the reservoirs or to maintain the direct supply to the Holy City.[1] The innumerable windings in the two longer aqueducts are due to the necessity of maintaining *a uniform level upon the hillsides* which are penetrated by many sub-valleys.

Here, then, are the constituent pieces of the puzzle. What are we to make of them?

I spent a whole fortnight studying this question from every conceivable angle, visiting the Pools frequently and exploring the still well-preserved remains of the numerous aqueducts. It would be inappropriate here to describe at length the many interesting archaeological facts which I encountered, but it is, I think, relevant to our present study to give the conclusions which I reached and to indicate briefly the line of reasoning which led to them. This will necessarily involve some discussion of the more outstanding features of the phenomena referred to.

I begin, therefore, with something which seems to me quite fundamental, viz. that whoever first built the Pools did so with the object of conveying the water for a considerable distance. In this respect the Pools and the aqueducts are logically inseparable. One cannot readily conceive of these great reservoirs being constructed at vast expense in a desolate and remote region like the Artas valley unless they were consciously designed for the purpose to which they were ultimately put.

1 It is much to be regretted that Dr. Schick's extremely interesting book on the water supply of Ancient Jerusalem is not available in an English translation. The details given in Plan 3 are based upon the data first made public in that work.

34. THE POOLS AND THE SPRINGS

An artist's impression of the Three Pools, showing the gradual descent of the reservoirs from the head of the valley

35. THE LOWEST POOL

looking down the Artas Valley (*right*) in the direction of Bethlehem

PLAN I

Showing the course of the three aqueducts to the north of the Pools of Solomon. It will be observed that the Low-Level Aqueduct connects the Pools with the famous rock cisterns beneath the Temple

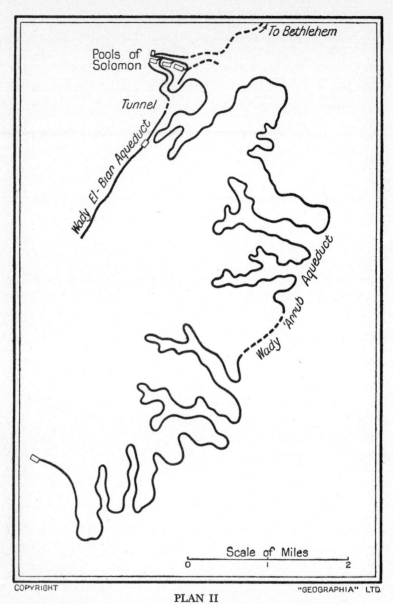

PLAN II

A companion diagram to Plan I, showing the two aqueducts which
brought water from the higher valleys to the vicinity of the Pools. The
High-Level Aqueduct to Jerusalem was a direct continuation of the
conduit from the Wady el-Biar

It would, perhaps, hardly be necessary to stress this view were it not that emphasis has been laid by some scholars upon a famous verse in the Book of Ecclesiastes in which Solomon appears to refer to the reservoirs:

> I made me gardens and orchards. I made me pools of water, to water therewith the wood that bringeth forth trees. (Eccles. 2, 5–6.)

Again in the Song of Songs (4, 12) we have the following significant sentence: "a garden enclosed is my sister, a spring shut up, a fountain sealed". It is generally recognized that the metaphor in this love passage is peculiarly appropriate to the 'Ain Saleh, the sealed spring to the west of the Castle.

There can be little doubt, indeed, that Solomon was rather fond of this quiet and restful retreat, for Josephus tells us in the *Antiquities* that:

> there was a certain place, about fifty furlongs distant from Jerusalem, which is called Etham; very pleasant it is in fine gardens and abounding in rivulets of water; thither did he [Solomon] use to go out in the morning. (*Ant.* 8, 7, 4.)

All these are very convincing little pen-pictures, but we must be careful to preserve our sense of proportion. Obviously the making of pools to *"water the wood which bringeth forth trees"* is a very different thing from the construction of great reservoirs which looked far beyond the needs of the Artas valley to the dense and growing population of Jerusalem itself. There is nothing in the sacred text or in the passage from Josephus which I have just quoted which suggests even remotely a consciousness of the prodigious feat of engineering which we are now considering. Rather does the reference of Josephus to "a valley abounding with rivulets" suggest the contrary.

I have personally, therefore, no alternative but to reject the suggestion put forward by Dr. Schick and some other early writers that the Pools were, as their name seems to imply, the work of Solomon.

In reaching this decision I am influenced by something which appears to me to be of final and conclusive weight. We have surely only to recall those hectic days when Hezekiah and his engineers were feverishly cutting the Siloam Tunnel. Solomon was long since dead and during those dread months of apprehension and political danger Hezekiah and his helpers had one supreme concern, viz. to *prevent Sennacherib from obtaining access to the water of the Virgin's Spring.* Of what possible use would that precaution have been if a great aqueduct carrying inexhaustible supplies from the Artas valley was ready to the invader's hand? The argument seems to me unanswerable. Whoever built the Pools and the aqueducts, it was certainly not the son of David.

With these considerations in mind I made careful inquiries in Jerusalem with a view to ascertaining whether there existed a reasonable consensus of opinion as to the probable date of the Pools.

I found that the diversity of view was not so great as I expected.

Dr. Sukenik, of the Hebrew University, who very

36. REMAINS OF HIGH–LEVEL AQUEDUCT

Taken from a point close to Rachel's Tomb

37. ANOTHER VIEW OF THE HIGH-LEVEL AQUEDUCT

Taken near Rachel's Tomb on the road to Bethlehem. Note the close fitting of the heavy stone sections

kindly gave me several hours of his valuable time, expressed the conviction that they are probably of Roman origin. This, of course, does not exclude their construction by Herod the Great, whose Roman pro-clivities are well known. Mr. P. L. O. Guy, who rendered me great service by placing the library of the British School of Archaeology at my disposal, drew attention to the P.E.F. Report, which records that "the general character of the masonry . . . resembles that of the Caesa-rea aqueducts and would seem, therefore, to be Roman work." Père Mamert Vionnet, who is an authority on the aqueducts and whose museum, the Notre Dame de France, has the best collection of stone blocks from the High-Level aqueduct, believes that the Low-Level channel, at least, was the work of Pontius Pilate.

Against this we have the opinion expressed by Sir George Adam Smith, whose judgments are not lightly to be disregarded, that the Pools and *one* of the aqueducts may have been in existence about a hundred years earlier since Timochares speaks of a city "running with water". Generally speaking, however, I found a marked tendency among contemporary scholars to attribute the Pools and their associated works to Herodian or later times.

We are compelled, therefore, to seek further light upon this subject by a careful study of the aqueducts them-selves.

Now if the reader will turn back to the plan on page 113 he will observe that the *lower* of the two Jerusalem aqueducts follows an extremely circuitous route as compared with its more elevated companion. There is, of course, a perfectly simple explanation. The Low-Level aqueduct, starting from the foot of the Pools, hugs the sides of the valleys, maintaining a uniform angle of descent throughout its entire course to the Holy City. Where an obstacle is interposed, as in the case of the hill of Bethlehem, a tunnel is constructed through it.

The High-Level aqueduct makes use of a somewhat different principle. Starting from a spring high up in the Wady Biar (see Plan 2) it circles the upper end of the Pools close to the site of the present castle. From here it drives for some miles direct towards its objective. Opposite Bethlehem it encounters a depression which it descends, rising again on the other side. These abrupt changes of level are made possible by the use of a sort of *inverted syphon*, constructed of square stone blocks so carefully joined together that they are not only watertight, but are capable of withstanding considerable pressure.

Many of these blocks or stone tubes have been removed to the local museums. One stands, as a sort of perpetual memorial, at the head of the Well of the Magi on the Bethlehem road (see Plate 38), but there is a very substantial section still *in situ* not far from Rachel's Tomb. I have given two photographs of this interesting exhibit.

We have thus two great aqueduct systems—obviously constructed at different periods—designed to bring water from the southern hills into Jerusalem. Both are examples of ancient engineering of a high order.

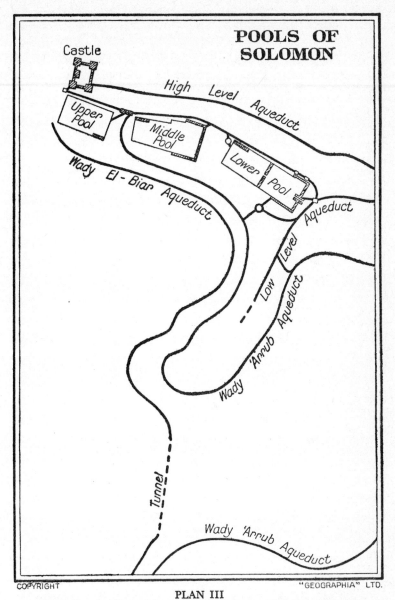

PLAN III

Exhibiting the ingenious way in which the water from the springs, the
feeder aqueducts and the Pools, were made to contribute to requirements
of Jerusalem. (Based upon drawing by Dr. Schick, 1810)

Which of these was the work of Pontius Pilate?

This, unfortunately, is a question to which no direct or immediate answer can be returned. There is, of course, one very definite clue which the historical student must take seriously into account. I mean the statement of Josephus that Pilate's aqueduct was at least *200 stadia in length.* Now the total distance traversed by the High-Level aqueduct from its source in the Wady-el-Biar to the point where it disappears abruptly near Mar Elias certainly does not exceed nine miles or approximately 72 stadia. Allowing for its possible extension to Jerusalem (say the Mamilla Pool) its total length would still be under 100 stadia.

Thus, on the testimony of Josephus—who is a reputable authority where the topography of Jerusalem is concerned —the High-Level aqueduct must definitely be ruled out.

When we turn, however, to the Low-Level aqueduct we get much more comparable results. The length of this aqueduct, *with all its windings,* from Jerusalem to the Pools of Solomon is approximately 21 miles. Again, with all its windings, the length of the 'Arrub conduit (above the Pools) is approximately 26 miles. Total length, 47 miles. This agrees so closely with the 400 stadia mentioned by Josephus in the *Jewish War* as to leave little doubt as to which system the historian had in mind.

I can see no point in casting needless discredit upon the accuracy of Josephus. Even if (as some believe) Herod the Great was the author of the 'Arrub sector of the aqueduct, leaving Pilate to complete the vital link between the Pools and the capital, it would still be true that Pilate "brought water" to Jerusalem and that he conducted it over a distance of 400 stadia.

The suggestion that Herod was directly associated with part of this great enterprise is supported in some degree by the assertion of Josephus that the Idumean conducted water to his stronghold at Herodium "from a great way off". Schick traced this aqueduct from the Artas spring (south of the Pools) to the ruins of the Castle. There is therefore concrete evidence that Herod was interested in this valley. It may well be that the whole grandiose scheme for supplying Jerusalem with water originated in his brain, but that its full and complete achievement was interrupted by his death. I cannot help feeling however, that those who would assign the entire work to him place an unreasonable burden upon the creative span of Herod's life. When we recall the gigantic achievement at Caesarea; the three great fortresses of Masada, Machaerus and Herodium; the rebuilding of Sebaste; and the colossal labours associated with his masterpiece, the third Temple at Jerusalem, need we wonder if this subsidiary task was left, either in embryo or in a state of only partial realization.

In view, therefore, of the definite statement of Josephus that Pilate brought water to Jerusalem from a distance of at least 200 stadia there are very strong reasons for believing that the Low-Level aqueduct is the work referred to.

What then of the Upper aqueduct?

I trust the reader will not think me presumptuous if here I definitely join issue with so great and respected an authority as Sir George Adam Smith. I have already paid tribute to the almost uncanny accuracy of his predictions and we are, of course, all very deeply in his debt. Long before I went out to Jerusalem, however, I was greatly perplexed by his very confident assertion that the High-Level aqueduct was the *older* of the two systems and was therefore already in existence when Pontius Pilate came upon the scene.

This seemed to me to be directly contrary to all those logical pointers which are the essence of sound historical reasoning. In the first place the diameter of the High-Level aqueduct is *fifteen* inches, whereas the average width of the Low-Level conduit is much smaller. The requirements of a great city like Jerusalem would naturally increase as time went on. One could understand the more limited supply being replaced or supplemented by the *less* limited, but hardly the reverse.

Secondly, the employment of the syphon principle to bridge the depression south of the so-called Plain of Rephaim suggests a more developed engineering technique than is observable in the lower channel. This would appear to indicate a later date. The very reason, too, which our author adduces for the priority of the High-Level aqueduct (viz. that it was necessary to feed the conduits and fountains of Herod's Palace) appeared to render superfluous the later construction of the Low-Level aqueduct altogether.

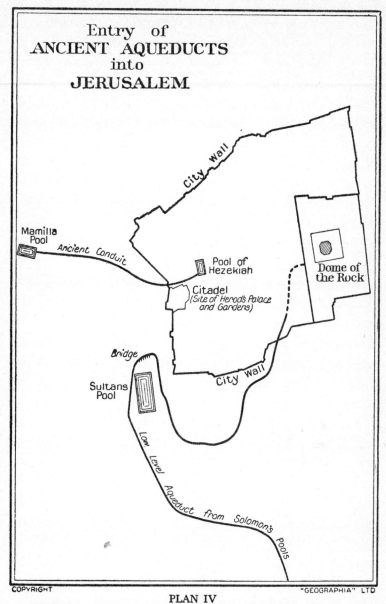

Entry of
ANCIENT AQUEDUCTS
into
JERUSALEM

Mamilla Pool

Ancient Conduit

City Wall

Pool of Hezekiah

Citadel
(Site of Herod's Palace and Gardens)

Dome of the Rock

Bridge

Sultans Pool

City Wall

Low Level Aqueduct from Solomon's Pools

PLAN IV

Showing the relation of the Mamilla Pool to the site of Herod's Palace.
An ancient conduit connected this pool with the Pool of the Patriarch's
Bath, believed by many authorities to be the "Amygdalon" of Josephus.
Reasons are given in the text for thinking that "deep canals" connected
this conduit with Herod's gardens

It is usually assumed by writers upon this subject that the destination of the High-Level aqueduct was the Mamilla Pool, which stands upon high ground to the north-west of the city (see Plan 4). An underground conduit connected this pool with the so-called Pool of Hezekiah within the precincts of Jerusalem. Now any one who has actually seen the Mamilla Pool and considered the delivery capacity of a fifteen-inch stone pipe will realize that, within a few hours, the pool would be filled to overflowing. A fraction of this supply would suffice for Herod's gardens and the storage capacity of Hezekiah's Pool (see Plate 52) is definitely limited. There would thus be an ample surplus to meet the needs of the Temple. Moreover, from this height it could be conducted to the Sanctuary enclosure very economically. Why, then, go to the vast labour and expense of building *another* conduit, forty-six miles in length, to supply almost exclusively the requirements of the Temple?

Finally, there is the very significant fact that one of the syphon blocks recovered from the High-Level aqueduct bears the inscription of a Roman Consul (Tineius Clemens) of the period of the Emperor Septimius Severus (A.D. 195). Sir George Adam Smith very properly draws attention to this inscription, but he argues that it can only indicate a work of *repair*, since, on his hypothesis, the aqueduct was needed to supply the conduits and fountains in Herod's Palace. Here again, however, the logical pointers lie in the opposite direction. One can understand the exposed sections of the aqueduct occa-

38. THE WELL OF THE MAGI
From immemorial times a welcome resting place on the road to Bethlehem.
The rectangular stone near which the donkeys are standing is a section taken
from the High-Level Aqueduct

39. SECTION OF THE WADY EL–BIAR AQUEDUCT

The old peasant is taking water for his small bed of eggplants

sionally needing attention and repair, but these massive stone tubes are so solid as to be practically indestructible. They would surely be the last sector of the conduit to require *complete replacement*. Indeed many of them have survived intact to this day.

So impressed was I by the cumulative force of these arguments that immediately after my return to London I wrote to Mr. John D. Whiting—a member of the American Colony and an archaeological student of long experience and repute—with a request that he should investigate the whole matter of the High-Level aqueduct afresh, with special reference to its probable destination in Jerusalem itself. It seemed to me that a profound mystery enveloped the inception of this famous conduit, and that, if possible, it should be cleared up before it is too late.

Mr. Whiting very kindly undertook this rather arduous task. He was at great pains to go over the ground again and subsequently sent me a long and extremely interesting report in which he describes how, in the light of this new experience, his previous belief and convictions had been profoundly modified.

In the course of his report Mr. Whiting stresses two facts which have tended to be overlooked in the earlier discussions. He points out that, according to Josephus, the tower *Hippicus* which adjoined Herod's Palace on the south-west hill, was solid to the height of thirty cubits, but *"above this solid and compact mass of masonry was a reservoir twenty cubits deep to receive rainwater"*. The existence of this great water tower, built by Herod himself and expressly designed to that end, would be quite inexplicable if, simultaneously, an inexhaustible supply of running or spring water had been available.

This incongruity is further emphasized by the testimony of the historian to the effect that *all* of the very numerous towers of the city had "upper chambers and cisterns to receive rainwater".

Thus the picture of Jerusalem presented to us, as rebuilt and fortified by Herod, is that of a city possessing few sources of living water and still mainly dependent upon the catchment and storage of the annual rainfall. Clearly at this period the High-Level aqueduct could not have been in sight.

But Mr. Whiting further directs our attention to the rather curious language in which Josephus refers to the gardens and fountains of Herod's Palace.

> All around were many circular cloisters, leading one into another, the columns in each being different, and their open courts all of greensward; there were groves of various trees intersected by long walks, which were bordered by *deep canals*, and ponds everywhere studded with bronze figures through which the water was discharged, and around the streams were numerous cots for tame pigeons. (*Jewish War*, V, 4, 4.)

Now the Greek word here rendered "canals", qualified, as it is, by the adjective "deep" clearly signifies something unusual. It suggests that a mere surface channel was not adequate and that a deep cutting had to be made before the water could be induced to flow.

Mr. Whiting finds this explicit reference to "deep canals" historically significant.

The reader will recall that an underground conduit connected the Mamilla Pool (see Plan 4) with the so-called Pool of Hezekiah at the head of a tributary of the Tyropean valley. Most scholars identify the last-mentioned pool with the "Amygdalon" of Josephus. To-day it is known to the Arabs as *Birket Hammam el-Batrak* or the Pool of the Patriarch's Bath.

Now the height of the top of the Mamilla Pool above the sea is 2,538 feet. It is nineteen feet deep, and the conduit starts from its base. The altitude of the sill of the Jaffa Gate, which is roughly level with the now-exposed foundations of Herod's Palace is 2,528 feet. Allowing for a slight dip the Mamilla conduit would thus pass Herod's Towers at a depression of from ten to twenty feet below the different levels of the Palace hill.[1]

This is a very reasonable figure for a cutting expressly characterized as "deep" and Mr. Whiting writes:

> If then the pool within the present city walls called Amygdalon has been proved ancient and the Mamilla Pool is supposedly Roman, and a canal of the ancient type connects them, is it not within reason to think that the continuation or branches of this Mamilla conduit were the deep canals that Josephus mentions, for deep they must have been. . . . The brazen statues "through which water ran out" could readily have been supplied by the cisterns in the towers or fed by cistern or canal water drawn up into special tanks."

[1] It is significant that in another passage Josephus speaks of "the gate through which water was taken to the tower of Hippicus."

In support of this suggestion it may be mentioned that there is no rock at these levels. The proposed deep canals could therefore easily be made. Some students report finding canals at the levels suggested.

What, then, of the High-Level aqueduct? Are we not as far from a solution as ever?

It is just here that Mr. Whiting's researches are of special interest. He stresses first the very strong evidence in favour of the belief that the stone syphon was the work of Roman legionaries, since the names of many centurions appear upon the blocks:

The first of these centurion names was found about 1800. De Saulcy discovered a number in 1861. The Notre Dame museum has quite a number of sections of this syphon, with the following centurion names on them: Antion, Vitalis, Clo(dius), Sat(urnin) Severi(twice), Pomponi(us), Quart(us) Flavianus, Sem(pronius), Flavi(anus). These are only a few of the many known. These names are roughly cut, just the work of an ordinary stone-chipper, and in some cases abbreviated, as above indicated. Each is preceded by a mark indicating the military rank of a centurion. The most interesting inscription in this Notre Dame collection of the actual stone sections, is of a consul who served in Palestine under the Emperor Septimius Severus in A.D. 195. (See *Jerusalem*, Sir Geo. Adam Smith, page 128.) It appears thus: Cos (Consul) I. Clement.

It is a recognized fact that this aqueduct is the work of Roman legionaries; at least all will agree that the syphon blocks are. The present writer, having found a section with the centurion name "Antion" some two to three hundred yards to the south of the one found thirty years ago, coupled with the fact that in the Notre Dame museum a centurion's name exists twice, believes that these inscribed stones are the beginning and end of a section constructed under the supervision of a single officer.

Secondly, Mr. Whiting emphasizes the well-known fact that no certain traces of this aqueduct have ever been found beyond the so-called Plain of Rephaim:

> Following this aqueduct north it abruptly ends on the up-grade opposite the Tantour grounds. Here is a large, very modern stone quarry cut clear across the course of the syphon. Had the aqueduct been buried here its end must surely show.
>
> Beyond Mar Elias (Greek Orthodox monastery of Elijah or Elias) on the so-called Plain of Rephaim, the present writer has often seen and, since beginning the present inquiry, carefully examined a section of masonry aqueduct running along the south side of the Bethlehem road. This is the farthest he has been able to follow this High-Level aqueduct. All the older authorities, who had a better chance before sections were destroyed, report not being able definitely to follow the aqueduct's course farther than hereabouts. (See G.A.S.—Jerusalem, page 128. Ordnance Survey of Jerusalem, 1865, page 83. Recovery of Jerusalem, pages 25 and 28.) Nor is it definitely certain that the bit above referred to belongs to the High-Level canal. Consensus of opinion is that it does.

The conclusion which Mr. Whiting reaches as a result of his investigations is that the High-Level aqueduct was begun by the Roman legionaries under the Emperor Septimius Severus but was actually never completed. He states his case thus:

> Let us then picture Jerusalem when it was Alia Capitolina. Here was a Roman garrison, a whole legion, every man a trained craftsman. There was no war to occupy them, and

we know the Roman officers believed in keeping their army busy. We have proofs of this through the explorations of Mr. C. N. Johns in their camp site on the south-west hill. Here Tenth Legion floor tiles and pottery water-pipes, with the Legion stamp impressed on them, have been found *in situ*.

In the Legion's quarters there were many cisterns and a canal supply from a rain pool. The amount would be prodigal for a palace but quite insufficient for a legion of soldiers and their horses and other animals. To keep them busy the idea was conceived of a better water supply, and Consul Clemens put his men to work. In the Department of Antiquities the High-Level aqueduct is referred to as "The Septimius Severus Aqueduct". Père Mamert Vionnet agrees to this.

I have presented these arguments at some length, and in the investigator's own words, because they will be generally regarded, I think, as putting very lucidly a personal viewpoint which must at least command attention and respect.

I am not competent to express a considered opinion upon this vexed question. It is for the local experts to decide, but I cannot help feeling that the answer to all our perplexities is really written quite plainly in the pages of Josephus.

After all, does not the historian expressly tell us that the Herodium aqueduct was built by Herod the Great and that Pontius Pilate "brought water" from a distance so clearly specified that it can only possibly refer to the Low-Level system? Had Herod also constructed the High-Level aqueduct, would not Josephus, with his admitted admiration for that monarch and his tendency to extol the architectural glories of Jerusalem, have mentioned so unique and ambitious a work?

I feel confident that he would.

That tribute, however, was denied him. When, in the reign of Septimius Severus, the Roman centurions set their mark upon the great stones of the High-Level aqueduct, Josephus had been dead for nearly sixty-eight years. If this be the case, then one thing is absolutely certain: the water which Pontius Pilate brought from the Artas valley to Jerusalem went into *the great cisterns beneath the Temple*. And that, as we shall see, is a fact of very considerable historical significance.

CHAPTER IX

PILATE SUPPRESSES A RIOT

Now it will be obvious to the reader that an engineering work of this magnitude, involving, as it did, vast structural changes in the vicinity of the Sanctuary itself, could not possibly have been undertaken without a great deal of prior discussion with the Jewish authorities. You could not, for example, have a situation in which Pilate suddenly arrived one morning with a huge baggage-train and an army of masons and proceeded forthwith to construct an aqueduct. The thing plainly called for a close and accurate survey of the whole site, and many problems affecting the Jewish administration and the civil rights of individuals must have arisen.

Thus the new aqueduct had to be carried by means of a specially constructed bridge over the valley of Hinnom. At one point it had to penetrate the city wall and at the vital junction with the sacred enclosure a channel had to be cut through the massive foundations of Herod's Temple. Not improbably some reconstruction or enlargement was necessary in the case of the existing rock cisterns in the Temple Mount.

All this implies consultation.

We have only to think of the dislocation caused, even in modern times, by the construction of a dock or the laying of a railway, to realize that, on and off, this ambitious project[1] must have been before Caiaphas and his fellow administrators for many months. Whether they approved of the scheme or not, they could hardly escape being involved in it. So much, at least, common sense and the history of colonial enterprises in all ages will teach us.

There are indications, however, that after the initial clash over the introduction of the ensigns a *modus vivendi* was reached between Pilate and the High Priest which enabled the business of state to be carried on with reasonable smoothness and without undue opposition from the Jewish leaders. That this is a true reading of the situation is demonstrated very clearly by the fact that *Pilate kept Caiaphas in office throughout the full period of his procuratorship.*

Now ten years is a very long time, during which in-

---

[1] The vast system of rock chambers cut in the Temple Mount for the storage of water was one of the most curious features of ancient Jerusalem. Of these thirty-six or thirty-seven are known and have been surveyed. "They may be distinguished [writes Sir George Adam Smith] into the smaller surface pits, arched over and probably not all originally cisterns, and the great deep basins hollowed out of the low-lying *meleki* rock, thirty, forty, fifty and sixty feet deep. One of them, the 'Great Sea', had a capacity of two million gallons. . . . Their enormous capacity was fed by the great aqueduct from Bethlehem. When they were full one can understand how even a very large garrison could face a siege without fear of a famine of water, while their besiegers suffered in the waterless environs" *Jerusalem*, Vol. I, p. 120). Schick (*Temple in Jerusalem*) attributes twenty-five of the cisterns, known at the present time by Jews as "the springs of the children of the prisons" to the Roman period.

numerable occasions would arise for an intolerant and domineering Governor to fall foul of the accredited representatives of the Jewish people. If Valerius Gratus could depose four High Priests in quick succession it was open to Pilate to adopt a similarly drastic course. Even the imperious Annas—a man of vast wealth and influence—had been forced to retire at the bidding of Valerius.

Given, therefore, a Procurator of really intractable temper, we should expect to find his affairs driving swiftly to a crisis, involving either the dismissal of Caiaphas or that far more formidable alternative, a rising of the people against Rome. On Philo's estimate of Pilate's character, it is doubtful whether even twelve months could have elapsed without an explosion.

Actually the situation seems to have been quite different.

Whatever criticisms may be levelled at the Jewish historian, the testimony of Josephus in this matter can hardly be doubted. Caiaphas was in office when Pilate first came to Caesarea. He was still there, ten years later, when the Procurator returned to Rome.

The maintenance of so delicate a poise between two men exercising wide authority in their respective spheres of influence implies that there existed between them some mutual understanding of each other's difficulties. Pilate could not hope to rule so turbulent a country as Judea without the active co-operation and advice of the High Priest. Conversely, Caiaphas was probably not averse to the Roman suzerainty, subject to the safeguard of his exclusive privileges and those of the circle to which he belonged. The defeat of the Romans, if it involved the advent of a political "Messiah", would not only have been embarrassing to these wealthy Sadduceans, but must have involved them in personal ruin.

At the very beginning, therefore, of the new Procuratorship, we can imagine Caiaphas using his diplomatic gifts to establish a sort of working concordat with Pilate. By birth and temperament he was destined to be a moderating influence in the councils of the nation and he could safely plead that it was in the interests of Rome to leave the taming of the more fiery spirits in the Jewish Assembly to him. If revolt threatened to raise its head he possessed wide powers for disciplining the offenders and, if necessary, to ensure delay.

In return the religious privileges of the Priesthood, which included a lucrative trade in the ceremonial requirements of the Temple, must be preserved.

Such, probably, was the basis of the understanding.

Caiaphas may not have put it quite so bluntly, but the essence of his pact with Pilate seems to have been this: "You keep to the political and administrative sphere and I will try to maintain the present uneasy state of national toleration of the Roman rule." It was a compromise at best—but it worked. Forty years were to elapse before the tyranny of later Governors and the fanaticism of the people brought the legions of Vespasian to Mount Scopus and ultimately laid Jerusalem, with all her glory, in the dust.

It is equally certain that the question as to who should pay for the vast expenditure in labour and material involved by the aqueduct must have been raised at a very early date.

Under the Roman system the financing of public works was usually provided for out of the revenue extracted from the people. In the case of Jerusalem, however, the situation was peculiar since an immense revenue was derived annually by the Temple authorities from the compulsory contribution of a half-shekel by every male adult member of the community. There was also a continual stream of wealth in the form of gold and votive offerings from Jews of the Dispersion. Edersheim computes that, at a moderate estimate, the combined income from these sources amounted to not less than £75,000 a year.

The first call upon this vast hoard, which for safety's sake was deposited in the Temple, was to defray the cost of those sacrifices which were made daily on behalf of the whole congregation, but the fund also maintained the entire fabric of the Temple, paid the salaries of a large staff, and met the cost of necessary repairs to the roads, streets and walls of the city. Even so, a considerable surplus remained.

There was, therefore, some justification for Pilate's insistence that the cost of the aqueduct should be defrayed out of this fund. Doubtless, from a religious and sentimental point of view, objections could be raised, but as a purely financial operation the proposal was legitimate, since the Jews of the Dispersion would thus help to glorify and enrich their beloved city. If the cost were not borne in this way, it would fall harshly in the form of increased taxes upon the local community. Caiaphas and his friends must have been fully alive to this point and while doubtless protesting strongly in principle, they seem finally to have acquiesced in the plan as the lesser of two evils. Certainly Pilate could not have raided the fund forcibly. The money (or its equivalent) must have been handed over to him with the official authority and consent of the High Priest.[1]

Immediately we view the matter in this light we begin to see that the incident so graphically described by Josephus was the logical outcome of such a situation. There is not a word in the passage printed on page 105 which suggests that the demonstration against Pilate was organized or led by the High Priest or indeed by any official nominee of the Great Sanhedrin. According to Josephus, the money from the Sacred Treasury had actually been expended. The authorities, therefore, were already implicated when, during the absence of Pilate, the news apparently leaked out. The populace was natur-

---

[1] In my earlier book, *Who Moved the Stone?* (first published over nine years ago) I suggested that "the question of finding the money for this very necessary public work would not have been difficult if put squarely to the authorities". In the much fuller light of the present inquiry it is clear that the question was put to them and that, reluctantly or otherwise, they agreed to a Temple grant. It was the indignation of the *populace* at this irregular proceeding which produced the riot.

ally furious and on the occasion of the Procurator's return, "the multitude . . . came about his tribunal and made a clamour about it".

Then follows a sentence which is very illuminating:

> Now when he [Pilate] *was apprised beforehand* of this disturbance he mixed his own soldiers in their armour with the multitude and ordered them to conceal themselves under the habits of private men, and not indeed to use their swords, but with their staves to beat those that made the clamour.

Who *warned Pilate beforehand* that there was going to be a commotion on his return to the capital?

It is possible, of course, that the guard at the fortress of Antonia may have heard rumours to this effect, but it is far more likely that Pilate's informant was Caiaphas. During the long drawn-out discussions upon the financial aspects of the aqueduct the High Priest must have argued very strongly the Jewish case that the Sacred Treasury was essentially a *religious fund* and could not properly be used for secular purposes. To this the Procurator would doubtless reply that the new aqueduct would provide additional supplies of water for the great cisterns beneath the Temple. When, therefore, the issue was finally settled and the consent of the Great Sanhedrin had reluctantly been given, Caiaphas could (and probably did) say to the Roman Procurator: "You have forced our hands in this matter. We will pay the money under protest but we cannot answer for the people. There is sure to be an uproar when news of this thing gets abroad."

138

And so, apparently, it turned out.

The storm broke during Pilate's absence in Caesarea and upon his return to Jerusalem a vast crowd assembled outside the Palace. Warned by his earlier experience the Procurator on this occasion acted with marked caution and restraint. He could not, of course, permit a hostile demonstration to go unchallenged in the very heart of the capital; neither could he conveniently condescend to *argue* with the populace, since the demonstration was really a protest against a decision secretly reached behind closed doors with their own leaders. On the other hand, to have used openly the military forces at his command would almost certainly have precipitated a conflict of a grave and far-reaching kind.

In these circumstances he adopted the expedient of *policing the crowds with members of the guard attired as civilians.* What then happened can perhaps best be inferred by a close comparison of the language used in the three separate versions of the incident which have descended to us.

It must be remembered that our extant copies of the works of Josephus do not go back beyond the eleventh century, and their survival is mainly due to Christian influences. During this period it was possible for vital passages dealing with disputed issues to undergo a change. Fortunately Eusebius, who was Bishop of Caesarea in the early part of the fourth century, gives numerous quotations from Josephus in his *Ecclesiastical History* and we have thus an early and independent check upon what the Jewish historian actually wrote.

Now Eusebius takes his extract from *The Jewish War* and it will be interesting to compare this version with the standard text given at the beginning of the preceding chapter:

> But after these things, he (i.e. Pilate) excited another tumult, by expending the public treasure which is called Corban, in the construction of an aqueduct. This extended nearly three hundred stadia (furlongs, i.e. from the city). The multitude were sorely grieved at it; and when Pilate came to Jerusalem, surrounding the tribunal, they began to cry out against him. But having anticipated their tumult, he planted his armed soldiers against the multitude, and previously intermixed them, concealed under the same common dress with the people. He had also forbidden them to use their swords, but ordered them to strike the noisy with clubs. The signal he gave from the tribunal. The Jews being thus beaten, many of them perished in consequence of the blows, many also being trodden to death by their own countrymen in the flight. The multitude, thus overawed by the misfortune of those slain, held their peace.

In order that no essential fact may be overlooked, let us now read the account of the incident, written by Josephus, eighteen years later, in the *Antiquities*:

> But Pilate undertook to bring a current of water to Jerusalem, and did it with the sacred money, and derived the origin of the stream from the distance of two hundred furlongs. However, the Jews were not pleased with what had been done about this water; and many ten thousands of the people got together, and made a clamour against him, and insisted that he should leave off that design. Some of them also used reproaches, and abused this man, as crowds of such people usually do. So he habited a great number of his soldiers in

their habit, who carried daggers under their garments, and sent them to a place where they might surround them. So he bade the Jews himself go away; but they boldly casting reproaches upon him, he gave the soldiers that signal which had been beforehand agreed on; who laid upon them with much greater blows than Pilate had commanded them, and equally punished those that were tumultuous, and those that were not; nor did they spare them in the least; and since the people were unarmed, and were caught by men prepared for what they were about, there was a great number of them slain by this means, and others of them ran away wounded; and thus an end was put to this sedition.

The reader will now have before him all that it is humanly possible to know about this celebrated incident. What conclusions are we to draw from these slightly varying accounts?

First and foremost, I think, we must recognize the fact that the demonstration against Pilate was of a strictly popular and democratic character. There is not even the remotest hint or suggestion that the High Priest in his official capacity was identified with it. Doubtless Caiaphas and his friends were secretly sympathetic to the cause of the rioters. They could hardly have been otherwise! But to have come forward at this late hour in an attempt to *undo a bargain to which, however reluctantly, they had previously given their consent*, would have been fatal to their interests.

Indeed, had Caiaphas officially backed this riot it is practically certain that it would have terminated his period of office. An alternative appointment would promptly have been made. Those ten years of unbroken ascendancy bear eloquent tribute to his skill in keeping on the right side of the Roman Governor.

This is clearly shown by the language of Josephus. In the *Jewish War* he tells us that it was the "multitude" which had "indignation" and came about the tribunal of Pilate. In the *Antiquities* he underscores the point by describing the mob, rather contemptuously, as abusing the Procurator "as crowds of such people usually do". Eusebius, who had the text of both works of Josephus before him, confirms this by stating that it was "the multitude" which was aggrieved and, when Pilate came to Jerusalem, surrounding the tribunal, "began to cry out against him".

We are thus plainly confronted by a situation of profound psychological interest. Pontius Pilate, following a sound Roman tradition, and acting, of course, strictly within his powers as *Procurator Caesaris* in Judea, decides to construct an aqueduct from the Pools of Solomon to the city. The cost of this in the ordinary way would have been raised by taxes upon the whole province, but since it was notorious that immense sums of money were contributed annually by the Jews of the Dispersion he decides that the expenses shall be defrayed from the Temple Treasury. The Jewish leaders demur very strongly, but rather than risk the consequences of open defiance of the Procurator they ultimately give way, and the first credits for the new aqueduct are paid out by the treasurers of the Temple fund.

Meanwhile news of this highly irregular transaction

has become public property, and is the subject of furious controversy in the synagogues and crowded bazaars of the city. Caiaphas warns Pilate that feeling is running high and that there is almost certain to be an angry demonstration when he returns—by which time the discordant elements will be multiplied and rendered more dangerous by the customary influx of large numbers of provincials for the Feast.

How does Pilate react to this situation?

He decides, quite rightly, that the open employment of the military would not only be highly inexpedient, but in the special nature of the circumstances uncalled for. He is not faced by an organized revolt, engineered by the leaders of Jewry, but by a discontented and fanatical populace. At all costs order must be maintained and the prestige of Rome upheld. He therefore gives orders for a selected body of men from the Roman fortress to attire themselves in civilian garb and to mix with the crowds converging on the Praetorium.

Now I think we can safely assume that no considerable body of Roman soldiers, with the limited wardrobe at their command, could have disguised themselves so effectively as completely to deceive the Jewish populace. The Semitic and Roman types were sharply distinguished and the seething crowds about the tribunal must have known that Pilate's supporters were present in force. What they were not prepared for was the seemingly excessive violence with which the latter interpreted their instructions.

Here Josephus, although a hostile witness, is meticulously fair to Pilate. He says in the *Jewish War* that the Procurator ordered the soldiers, "not indeed to use their swords, but with their staves to beat those that made the clamour". Eusebius emphasizes the explicit character of this instruction: "He had forbidden them to use their swords, but ordered them to strike the noisy with their clubs." Finally Josephus, reviewing the whole business many years later in the *Antiquities*, confesses that the soldiers laid about them "with much greater blows than Pilate had commanded them, and equally punished those that were tumultuous and those that were not".

We can readily picture the scene.

Pilate has returned to Jerusalem and is in residence once more at the Praetorium. There are some minor cases to be tried and arrangements have been made for a tribunal to be set up in the open courtyard. Meanwhile the officers and men of the great fortress of Antonia are astir early. As dawn breaks over the Mount of Olives a parade is held and the centurions select a picked body of men for policing the crowds which are expected to gather. The instructions are explicit: civilian dress will be worn and all arms concealed. If, however, the crowd threatens to become unmanageable, the soldiers are to quieten the ringleaders with their clubs. The really insurgent and rebellious members of the crowd are to be taught a lesson.

As the morning wears on it becomes evident that the

40. STREET SCENE
The Ecce Homo Arch, looking west

41. CROWDS IN DAVID STREET
One of the busiest thoroughfares in the Old City

task of these men is going to be very difficult. The vast crowd, packed tight in the courtyard of the Palace, is much greater than was expected, and the Romans are outnumbered many times. There is a mighty shout as Pilate at last makes his appearance at the tribunal, and for a few moments pandemonium reigns. Offensive epithets are hurled at the Procurator, fists are shaken in angry defiance and, at a prearranged signal, a number of local brawls start simultaneously, as his supporters trounce the more vocal of their opponents.

In an Oriental city under Roman domination there could be only one result of such a clash between the rival partisans of two conflicting systems.

Doubtless the Romans, stung by the insults heaped publicly upon their superior officer, exceeded the instructions which Pilate had caused to be given to them. Tempers rose rapidly as the surprised demonstrators tried to fight back against their armed assailants, but in a few moments panic had seized the vast gathering. The exits from the square were probably few and certainly very narrow. Only the more fortunate of the demonstrators situated on the outskirts of the crowd, would be able to make their way to a place of safety. These exits would swiftly be choked, and for the rest there would be all the terrors of a stampede in a confined space. To stumble, or even to falter, would be to be borne down and to be trampled underfoot.

Such clearly is the picture which Josephus presents to us when he records that, while many died of the blows which they received, "many others perished as trodden to death by themselves".

When the square was at length cleared and the crowds slowly filtered back into the lower city it was seen that the insurgent movement had collapsed. "The multitude, astonished at the calamity of those that were slain, held their peace."

It is thus abundantly clear from our extant records of this famous incident that we are here dealing, not with an organized and direct protest from the Jewish leaders, but with the *popular backwash* of a rather strained political situation in which the High Priest and his associates had been compelled, very reluctantly, to give way under strong pressure from their Roman overlord.

Reviewing the situation quietly in his apartments that evening, Caiaphas may secretly have had some cause for satisfaction. The peace of the realm had been purchased at a price and a very dangerous corner in his official career had been successfully negotiated. Time would bring its revenge for any humiliation which he had personally suffered.

Meanwhile he was free to devote his attention to another and very different problem which was already giving the authorities in Jerusalem some concern. For *things were happening just then in Galilee and on the other side of the Jordan which called for close watching*. By this time Caiaphas may have flattered himself that he knew how to handle the Roman Procurator, but the menace which was now brewing might well prove in the upshot to be beyond even his diplomacy and skill. Was it not written in the Book of Malachi:

> Behold I will send my messenger and he shall prepare the way before me, and the Lord whom ye seek shall suddenly come to his temple, and the messenger of the Covenant whom ye delight in; Behold, *he shall come*, saith the Lord of Hosts.

CHAPTER X

THE THIRD INVESTIGATION

I said in an earlier chapter that there are two fundamentally divergent views concerning the true character
of the situation in Jerusalem during the fatal Passover
which witnessed the arrest, trial and crucifixion of Jesus
of Nazareth.

It would, perhaps, be more accurate to say that they
are diametrically opposed.

The most familiar picture is that presented to us in
the pages of the four Gospels. It would, of course, be
quite untrue to say that the Gospels are agreed upon all
points in connection with that tragedy. They differ frequently in matters of detail and a complete harmony
cannot be established between them. In this they appear
to me to conform to normal human experience. It is very
rarely that three or more independent accounts of the
same event, although written in good faith, achieve a perfect unanimity. Indeed, in certain contingencies, such
agreement might seriously impair the evidential value of
the witness.

It *is* true, however, to say of the Gospels that they

present a solid and united front on some vital matters affecting the dramatic *tempo* and the general atmosphere surrounding the tragedy. They all agree, for example:

(*a*) That Pilate was in Jerusalem for the Feast, and one Gospel assures us that on this occasion he brought his wife with him.

(*b*) That Jesus was betrayed by one of His own followers on the evening before the Crucifixion.

(*c*) That He was arrested late at night in the Garden of Gethsemane and brought to preliminary trial at the instance of the Jewish authorities.

(*d*) That the same authorities found Him guilty of death and sought ratification of this sentence from Pontius Pilate.

(*e*) That Pilate, after a further hearing of the case, emphatically demurred, but under strong pressure from the Priests, ultimately gave way.

There are, of course, many other points upon which the Gospels are in substantial agreement—such, for example, as the statement that, after the execution of the sentence, Pilate gave authority to a leading member of the Jewish hierarchy to arrange for the proper burial of the body. I have selected these five basic features, however, because they set, as it were, the pace of the drama. They are linked together in a definite and quite logical sequence of time, and they cannot be disturbed without transforming radically the political complexion of the whole matter.

I think it was the late Lord Balfour who declared, with profound truth, that a book *never wholly shakes off its first draft.* However much the author may try to modify its contents or adapt its message to new circumstances, certain fixed and ineradicable features remain. Most professional writers will heartily endorse this dictum and it seems to me that in these five points we have the ineradicable residuum—the things upon which everybody was agreed who had personally passed through that harrowing experience.

There is, however, an alternative and quite different version of the circumstances surrounding the Great Tragedy. The essence of this view is that the events which culminated in the arrest and crucifixion of Jesus were fundamentally *revolutionary* in character; that they involved the employment of armed force; and that, willingly or otherwise, Jesus of Nazareth was involved in the consequences of an abortive insurrection aimed at the establishment of a Messianic régime.

As we shall see presently there are passages in the Gospels themselves which at first sight seem to lend support to this hypothesis which has been put forward by various modern writers[1] of whom, perhaps, the most

[1] The suggestion that there was a revolutionary background to the Gospel story is, of course, by no means confined to modern times. As early as A.D. 220, Sossianus Hierocles, governor of Phoenicia and other places in the vicinity of Palestine declared that Jesus, "having been routed by the Jews, committed acts of brigandage (latrocinia) at the head of a band of nine hundred men". Lactantius, who has preserved this statement, tells us that Hierocles was reasoning "not against but *for* the Christians" and would be unlikely, therefore, to make any statement which was not at least widely believed to be true. Celsus (quoted by Origen, *In Celsum*, viii, 14) makes a somewhat similar accusation. See also article by H. P. Kingdon, M.A., entitled "Had the Crucifixion a Revolutionary Significance?" *Hibbert Journal*, Vol. 35, No. 4. 1937.

representative is Dr. Robert Eisler, sometime professor at the University of Leipzig and Guest-Lecturer at the Sorbonne in Paris. Dr. Eisler is a classical student with a profound knowledge of the literature of the early Christian era, and about thirty years ago his interest was aroused by the then newly discovered Slavonic version of the *Jewish War* which contains an account of the arrest and crucifixion of Jesus of Nazareth—a phase of Pilate's story upon which Josephus, in the standard text of that work, is completely silent.

For reasons which I shall give later, Dr. Eisler formed the opinion that what Josephus originally wrote upon this subject was so damaging to the Church that it was altered by the Christians in such a manner as to convey an entirely different meaning. Later when Christianity was triumphant, under the Emperor Constantine, the offensive passages were expunged altogether.

Now we may agree at once that any reasoned explanation of the silence of Josephus demands our closest attention and when Dr. Eisler's book first appeared in 1931 I read it through very carefully. It is generally agreed that the preservation of the works of the Jewish historian is largely due to Christian influence and it seemed to me at least a defensible proposition that in the course of centuries, at the hands of copyists, the text may have suffered some change. The method of determining the extent of these changes is, of course, highly subjective and must be used with scrupulous care.

Dr. Eisler has his own peculiar critical apparatus for

disentangling the supposed Christian alterations from what he regards as the original script of Josephus. I shall give examples of this in the next chapter. It will help us, however, to appreciate better the main issues if we postpone for the moment consideration of the intermediate stages of the argument and plunge straight into the conclusions which Dr. Eisler reaches.[1]

We must think therefore of Jerusalem, on the eve of the fatal Passover, as being in a state of panic and grave social disorder. Rather unexpectedly Pontius Pilate is at Caesarea with the main body of the Roman army. The great fortress of Antonia is temporarily in the hands of the Temple guard. A Roman cohort, consisting of about five hundred or six hundred men, "with a squadron of Samaritan cavalry", is in occupation of Herod's Palace on the western hill. This small force, while strong enough to hold the Palace, is quite inadequate to deal with a situation of a more formidable kind.

On the Sunday morning immediately preceding the Feast such an emergency arises.

Among the vast body of pilgrims which have for some days been converging upon the capital is a subversive element consisting chiefly of Galileans, inspired by the revolutionary teaching of Jesus of Nazareth. These disaffected elements assemble secretly on the Mount of Olives and proclaim Jesus king.

---

[1] The citations from Eisler given in these pages are taken from the English translation of his monumental work by Dr. Alexander Krappe: *The Messiah Jesus and John the Baptist*, Methuen, London 1931.

About a thousand men, preceding or following their leader, enter the city. "The prophet is carried forward by the ever-increasing pressure of the crowd into the temple, suddenly occupied by surprise by men carrying hidden arms. The Levitic guard offers no resistance. . . ." The temple with its castle of Antonia, then without a Roman garrison, falls into the hands of the Galileans. Meanwhile "the *Barjonim* of Jerusalem, who have made common cause with the insurgents, surprise the guards and seize the Tower of Siloam", a defensible fortress in the south-east corner of the city.

Alarmed by these grave manifestations of revolt, the messengers sent by the military tribunes of Herod's castle vie with those of the High Priest in "warning the Governor in far-off Caesarea of what had taken place and in clamouring for the speedy despatch of his legion". Pilate approaches "in forced marches". By Thursday, the day of the preparation, the rebellion is repressed, the temple "reconquered in the same manner in which it had been taken—that is, by a band of apparently peaceful pilgrims". The blood of the Galileans is thus mingled with their sacrifice. (Luke xiii, 1). The Tower of Siloam, laid low by the Roman battering rams "cover the corpses of eighteen of the rebellious Jerusalemites". (Luke xiii, 4.)

In the stillness of the night, "a few hours after the sounds of the *Hallel* announced the end of the Passover meal, a Roman cohort, increased by a guard of loyalists hurriedly armed by the high priests with clubs and daggers" surround the Mount of Olives. After a weak

153

attempt at resistance, given up almost immediately by the express command of Jesus, "the leader of the revolt —in Roman eyes only the one-day king of a belated and bloody *Saturnalia*—is captured, promptly condemned that same night according to martial law, and crucified along with two other 'robbers', leaders of the insurrection."

Such briefly is the hypothetic situation extracted by Dr. Eisler from the Slavonic Josephus. I have described it with some care, and as far as possible in the critic's own words because I am sincerely anxious not to distort or to present a misleading version of what he says. Profoundly as one may differ from his final conclusions Eisler has produced a book which not only challenges some of the deepest convictions of the Christian faith but which, by reason of its highly documented character, must necessarily leave a mark upon the critical history of our time. Mere polemics are here out of place. Only by a conscientious investigation of the facts can we arrive at the basic and underlying truth.

CHAPTER XI

IN WHICH A JEWISH SCHOLAR PROPOUNDS A RATHER STARTLING THEORY

How, then, does Dr. Eisler reach these conclusions?

First and foremost—and this is really the bed-rock of his theory—Eisler believes that shortly after the Crucifixion, Pontius Pilate, in his official capacity as Roman Governor, sent a report upon the case to the Emperor Tiberius and that this was preserved with the official records in the *tabularium principis* at Rome.

It is well known that, in consequence of his services to Vespasian and Titus, Josephus rose to high favour with the Flavian House. He was given facilities to study under Imperial patronage and while in Rome produced the bulk of his literary output including, of course, his great work, the *Antiquities*.

Now the *Jewish War* was first published by Josephus about the year A.D. 72. It appeared in two forms: a Greek edition for the Roman public and an earlier draft in Aramaic, entitled *On the Capture of Jerusalem*. This latter title was doubtless chosen to make it more acceptable to Jewish readers, since the historian tells us in the preface that he composed the work in his own "vernacular tongue".

Without, of course, having any actual documentary proof of his contention, Dr. Eisler takes it for granted that, during his researches into the Procuratorship of Pontius Pilate, Josephus had access to the Imperial records and that he found therein, among other relevant documents, Pilate's official note on the case, giving the grounds for the conviction, and a sheet which he calls a "hue-and-cry" notice—being a sort of "police report" (his own words) issued prior to the arrest and containing a personal description of the wanted man.

In his book, which is very fully documented, Dr. Eisler prints an interesting example of a writ relating to two fugitive Alexandrian slaves, accused of theft in the year 145 B.C. Like its modern counterpart this writ embodies a detailed description of the physical appearance of each fugitive:

> Of medium height, beardless, straight-legged, with a dimple in the chin, a mole to the left of his nose, a scar above the left angle of his mouth, tattooed on the right wrist . . . whoever brings back this fellow shall receive two talents of brass. If he is denounced after reaching the asylum of a sanctuary, one talent. If shown to be in the hands of a solvent and responsible person, three talents. Information may be given by anyone to the chief magistrate's officers.

Eisler stresses the well-known fact that in the Fourth Gospel we are expressly told that the chief priests and Pharisees "had given a commandment that if any man knew where he [Jesus] were, he should show it, that they might take him". (John xi, 57). And he argues that the various "descriptions of Christ" which undoubtedly circulated during the early Christian era really derived from the publication of a document of this kind.

Of these "descriptions" of the physical appearance of Jesus the most famous is the so-called "Letter of Lentulus", a document of rather unusual interest. Since many of my readers may not be familiar with the text I print it below in the late Dr. M. R. James's admirable English translation:

There has appeared in these times and still is a man, if it is right to call him a man, of great virtue, called Christ whose name is Jesus, who is said by the Gentiles to be a prophet of truth, whom his disciples call Son of God, raising the dead and healing all diseases: a man of stature tall, medium, i.e. fifteen palms and a half and slightly, having a venerable face which beholders might love and dread, having hair of the colour of an unripe hazel and smooth almost to the ears, but from the ears down corkscrew curls, somewhat darker coloured and more glistening, waving downwards from the shoulders, having a parting on the middle of his head after the manner of the Naziraeans, a brow smooth and most serene, with a face without a wrinkle or spot, beautified by a ruddy colour; with nose and mouth there is no fault whatever. Having a beard copious but immature of the same colour as the hair, not long but parted in the middle. Having a simple and mature aspect, with blue eyes of varying hue and bright. In rebuke terrible, in admonition bland and amiable. Cheerful, yet preserving gravity: he sometimes wept but never laughed. In stature of body tall and erect, having hands and arms delectable to the sight. In converse, grave, sweet and modest, so that justly according to the prophet was he called beauteous above the sons of men.

At first sight this document does not appear to bear much resemblance to the Alexandrine writ quoted above but, as Eisler says, the letter was undeniably produced in the Christian interest and he claims that, like an ancient palimpsest, traces of its original character—the Balfourian "first draft"—show through.

He demonstrates this by suppressing what he regards as the "Christian interpolations" and setting the more significant words in black type, thus:

> a man of stature . . . fifteen palms and a half . . . having a face which beholders might . . . dread, having hair . . . having a parting in the middle of his head after the manner of the Naziraeans, with nose. . . . Having a beard . . . immature . . . parted in the middle. Having a simple and mature aspect, etc.[1]

So much, then, for the description of the physical appearance of Jesus. Let us now proceed a stage further.

In the course of his argument Dr. Eisler emphasizes the fact that the *titulus* which Pilate caused to be nailed to the cross of Jesus bore the significant words: "*The King of the Jews*". This of course is the unanimous testimony of the four Gospels. Even if intended ironically this phrase could hardly have been written save as the result of some kind of legal process in which it was sought to fasten on the prisoner the guilt of having aspired to the

---

[1] The Letter of Lentulus follows very closely the traditional portraits of Christ. In its present form, however, according to Dr. James, the document can hardly be older than the thirteenth century and was probably written in Italy.

throne and, in the full political sense, such an aspiration could, of course, only be realized by resort to violence.

Now Dr. Eisler holds that, embedded in the language used by the Gospel writers, there lie certain traces of a revolutionary movement of this character. In his submission this movement first began to obtain popular support as the direct result of the teaching of John the Baptist, whom he describes as a sort of "field chaplain" to the scattered forces which were ultimately to put their convictions to the test. He directs our particular attention to the Greek word translated "soldiers" in the following extract from St. Matthew's Gospel:

> And soldiers also asked him, saying: And we, what must we do? And he said unto them, Do violence to no man, neither exact anything wrongfully; and be content with your wages.

He contends that this could not possibly have referred to the Roman legionaries and that the word is more accurately rendered: "people on the war-path". The whole passage (obviously derived by St. Matthew from some earlier source) appears to Eisler to be a fairly close and faithful report of a "field-sermon" delivered by this ardent "revolutionary" to his rather ill-disciplined followers. In support of this the critic quotes the famous saying attributed to Jesus in St. Matthew xi, 12:

> From the days of John the Baptist until now the kingdom of heaven suffereth *violence* and men of violence *take it by force.*

Then there are the very curious passages in the Gospels

in which reference is made to *swords*. The first of these occurs in St. Matthew (Ch. 10, v. 34) in which Jesus is reported as saying: "Think not that I come to send peace on the earth. I came not to send peace, but a sword." The second is in St. Luke (Ch. 22, v. 35–6):

> And he said unto them, When I sent you forth without purse, and wallet, and shoes, lacked ye anything? And they said, Nothing. And he said unto them, But now, he that hath a purse, let him take it, and likewise a wallet: and he that hath none, let him sell his cloke and buy a sword. . . . And they said, Lord, behold here are two swords. And he said unto them, It is enough.

The third is in St. Mark's account of the betrayal (Ch. 14, v. 47):

> But a certain one of them that stood by *drew his sword* and smote the servant of the High Priest and struck off his ear.

Dr. Eisler concludes from these passages that Jesus secretly armed his followers before leading them to Jerusalem. Finally, there is the article "the" in most of the Greek manuscripts of St. Mark's Gospel where the Evangelist refers to Barabbas as:

> lying bound with them that had made insurrection, men who in *the* insurrection had committed murder.

This specific reference to an armed revolt without any apparent consciousness of the need for further indentification is held by Eisler to indicate that the insurrection was well remembered as the one which ultimately cost Jesus his life.

160

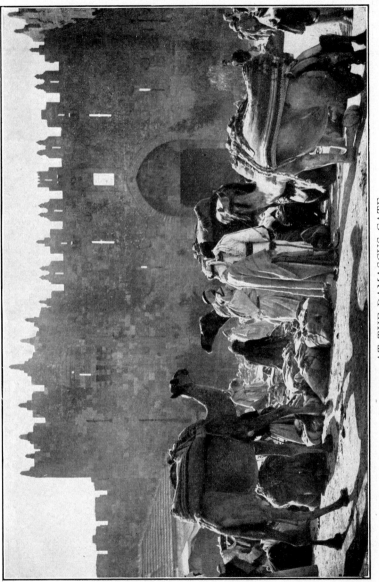

42. AT THE DAMASCUS GATE

Early morning scene at the most famous gate of the ancient city

43. "SOLOMON'S STABLES"
Part of the immense substructure on the Temple Mount

From these general considerations our critic proceeds to a close study of the "Jesus passage" in the now famous Slavonic version of Josephus. I have printed this passage in full on a separate page. The reader may study it at his leisure. It is sufficient for our immediate purpose to quote the two final paragraphs:

> And they went and communicated the matter to Pilate and he sent and had many of the multitude slain. And he had that wonder-worker brought up and after instituting an enquiry concerning him pronounced judgment: He is a bene-factor, not a malefactor, nor a rebel, nor covetous of kingship. And he let him go, for he had healed his dying wife.
>
> And he went to his wonted place and did his wonted works. And when more people again assembled round him, he glori-fied himself through his actions more than all. The teachers of the Law were overcome with envy, and gave thirty talents to Pilate, in order that he should put him to death. And he took it and gave them liberty to execute their will themselves. And they laid hands on him and crucified him contrary to the law of their fathers.

All this is, of course, abject nonsense which finds no support in the far earlier tradition of the Gospels. The statement that Jesus had healed the dying wife of Pilate is a very late legend indeed, while the suggestion that the priests bribed Pilate with thirty talents could only have been written by some one who had either never heard of Judas Iscariot or to whom the facts had come down in a very garbled form. Certainly Josephus, proud of his Levitical descent and thoroughly familiar with the legal procedure of his country, would not have com-mitted the blunder of suggesting that the Jews *crucified*

FULL TEXT OF THE "JESUS" PASSAGE
FROM THE SLAVONIC JOSEPHUS

At that time there appeared a man, if it is permissible to call him a man. His nature and form were human, but his appearance was something more than that of a man; notwithstanding his works were divine. He worked miracles wonderful and mighty. Therefore it is impossible for me to call him a man; but again, if I look at the nature which he shared with all, I will not call him an angel. And everything whatsoever he wrought through an invisible power, he wrought by word and command. Some said of him, "Our first lawgiver is risen from the dead and hath performed many healings and arts", while others thought he was sent from God. Howbeit in many things he disobeyed the law and kept not the Sabbath according to our fathers' customs. Yet, on the other hand, he did nothing shameful; nor did he do anything with aid of hands, but by word alone did he provide everything.

And many of the multitude followed after him and hearkened to his teaching; and many souls were in commotion, thinking that thereby the Jewish tribes might free themselves from Roman hands. Now it was his custom in general to sojourn over against the city upon the Mount of Olives, and there, too, he bestowed his healings upon the people.

And there assembled unto him of ministers one hundred and fifty, and a multitude of the people. Now when they saw his power, that he accomplished whatsoever he would by a word, and when they had made known to him their will, that he should enter into the city and cut down the Roman troops and Pilate and rule over us, he disdained us not.

And when thereafter knowledge of it came to the Jewish leaders, they assembled together with the High Priest and spake: "We are powerless and too weak to withstand the Romans. Seeing, moreover, that the bow is bent, we will go and communicate to Pilate what we have heard, and we shall be clear of trouble, lest he hear it from others, and we be robbed of our substance and ourselves slaughtered and our children scattered." And they went and communicated it to Pilate. And he sent and had many of the multitude slain. And he had that wonder-worker brought up, and after instituting an inquiry concerning him, he pronounced judgement: "He is a benefactor, not a malefactor, nor a rebel, nor covetous of kingship." And he let him go; for he had healed his dying wife.

And he went to his wonted place and did his wonted works. And when more people again assembled round him, he glorified himself through his actions more than all. The teachers of the Law were overcome with envy, and gave thirty talents to Pilate, in order that he should put him to death. And he took it and gave them liberty to execute their will themselves. And they laid hands on him and crucified him contrary to the law of their fathers.

Jesus. Had the priests been given *carte blanche* in this matter they would, undoubtedly, have *stoned* him, as later they did Stephen and other martyrs of the early Church.

Precisely, says Dr. Eisler in effect.

These obviously untrustworthy and absurd elements are late Christian interpolations. Remove them—and at the same time delete everything which plainly conflicts with the hostile attitude of Josephus towards Jesus—and you will at once see the clear outline of the original text showing through.

Eisler draws particular attention to the reported verdict of Pilate:

> "He is a benefactor, not a malefactor, nor a rebel, nor covetous of kingship."

It is easy to recognize (he writes) that the word "benefactor" and the particles "not . . . nor . . . nor", which are "historically so improbable, are not wanted in the sentence quoted above and have been interpolated by an indignant Christian to correct what was to him an intolerable statement. If these words be omitted we are left with a plausible verdict:

> "He is a malefactor . . . a rebel . . . thirsting to be king."

I have said enough, I hope, to illustrate the basic principle by which Eisler extracts from the records his theory of an armed insurrection, in the course of which Pilate is hastily summoned to the capital and has to recapture the Temple and certain strategic positions associated with it.

It remains only to add one rather vital fact, viz. that the Slavonic or Old Russian version of the *Jewish War*, upon which this reconstruction is mainly based, has come down to us in seventeen manuscripts of the fifteenth and sixteenth centuries. Eisler believes that these versions are based upon copies of the early draft by Josephus entitled "On the Capture of Jerusalem", which, by some accident, *escaped expurgation.* Thus, he argues, we have an adequate explanation of one of the strangest facts in ancient literature; *the silence of the "Jewish War" about the tragedy of Christ.*

CHAPTER XII

THE REAL CRUX OF THE PROBLEM

EARLY one morning towards the close of my stay in Jerusalem, I asked Lusho Fath'ullah to fetch the car, since I was anxious to pay another visit to the Pool of Siloam.

There is no motor road to the junction of the three valleys near which the Pool lies. So we parked the Hillman high up, close to the south-west angle of the city wall and scrambled down the precipitous slope on foot. The pathway is stony and uneven. Often we had to stand aside while heavily laden donkeys or a party of women with baskets on their heads, passed us on the ascent, bearing fruit and vegetables from the gardens below.

Above us, to the left, rose the mighty walls of the Haram-es-Sherif or sacred enclosure, within which stands the Noble Sanctuary, the historic and exquisite mosque known as the Dome of the Rock—a fitting successor to the three great temples of Jewish times. More than once I turned to look round at this towering curtain of stone against the morning sky, and tried to recapture the thrill which every provincial visitor to Jerusalem must have felt as he looked up the Tyropean valley to the rich and fabulously costly structure of Herod's Temple on the Mount.

Presently the gradient slackened and within a few minutes we reached the Pool. A flight of steps leads down to the basin, which to-day is rectangular in shape and measures approximately 59 ft. x 18 ft. At the north-east corner there is a roughly hewn cutting in the rock (see Plate 33). This is Hezekiah's tunnel through which water still flows from the Virgin's Spring. A bundle of clothes lay upon the stone flags and from the darkness of the cavity came the happy laughter of boys, splashing and playing in the fresh, limpid stream.

They were probably far too young to realize the tense excitement which must have prevailed at that very spot on the morning when Hezekiah and his engineers first saw the water making its appearance through the rock. Even to us, it is just history, but to those early dwellers in Jerusalem it must have been an occasion for great jubilation. Temporarily, at least, Sennacherib had been foiled. Next time the Assyrian came that way he would not find things quite so easy.

There are, of course, other associations with this deeply fascinating spot.

It was here that a certain blind man was sent by the Prophet of Nazareth, with express instructions to bathe his eyes in the stream—and having great faith was healed. Here, too, Jesus Himself must often have paused, watching the children play and the women filling their pitchers, preparatory to the long climb back to the city. Nowhere, perhaps, save amid the gnarled and ancient trees of the Garden of Gethsemane, can you be more certain that you are standing within a few feet of the soil He trod.

On this occasion, however, I set these softer and more personal memories aside. I had come here upon a much more practical errand, viz. to test a vital link in Dr. Eisler's theory.

Somewhere very near this spot must have stood the structure which St. Luke refers to as "the Tower in Siloam". Possibly it was one of the many towers which Josephus tells us rose at intervals from the walls of the old city. In this case it stood a short distance to the south where the researches of Dr. Bliss have traced an ancient rampart crossing the foot of the Tyropean valley and climbing steeply up the side of Ophel. Perhaps Dr. Eisler's own conjecture is right and the ruins of an ancient building close to the Jebusite fortress, discovered in 1920 by Major Raymond Weill, is the base of this celebrated tower.

What does it really matter?

Within fifty to a hundred paces of the spot where Lusho and I then stood rose the "Tower in Siloam" and that was all I needed for the moment. I had come here, not to excavate, but to *reflect*, with all the splendour of that incomparable scene before me.

I looked up at the mighty platform upon which Herod's

Temple once stood—dominated by the austere and gloomy castle of Antonia—and thought how very strange it was that, during this particular feast, that vital key to the temple fortress of Jerusalem should have been in *Jewish* hands!

And the more vivid the contemporary scene grew, the clearer it became that Dr. Eisler's theory would have been much stronger than it is if he had not succumbed to the temptation to associate the death of the "eighteen Galileans" referred to by St. Luke with the tragedy of Jesus.

For consider what it means.

It is an essential part of Eisler's proposal that the insurrection was sufficiently successful to enable the Galileans to capture and hold, not merely the Temple and its courts, but certain strategic defences of the capital, and he searches the Gospels for stray hints which will support this hypothesis. He comes across the reference of Jesus to the untimely fate of eighteen Galileans who perished as a result of the collapse of the Tower in Siloam. He argues (quite reasonably) that strong towers do not collapse of their own weight. He therefore adopts, rather eagerly, the precarious suggestion that the tower fell to the *battering rams of Pilate*.

Now Dr. Eisler knows far too much about Jerusalem and the Roman methods of governing their far-flung empire to believe that, had Pilate been in residence in the capital, a mere thousand relatively untrained Galileans could have established themselves in the

Temple courts. The legionaries would have descended swiftly into the arena and put an end to the whole business.

He is therefore compelled to make two further assumptions:

(1) That the fortress of Antonia, which commanded the Sanctuary, was occupied at this period by the *Temple Guard*.

(2) That Pilate was in *Caesarea*, "enjoying himself quietly in the delights which that relatively civilized city offered to a gentleman of his class"—a sort of historic anticipation of Nero's fiddling while Rome burned.

Incidentally the reader can hardly miss a certain unconscious irony in the suggestion of Pilate's *inactivity*. We hear so much in the literature of his bustling and assertive character, his interference in things which did not concern him, his brutality, his harsh and iron rule, that this picture of him dallying at ease in Caesarea is at least unusual.

The suggestion, too, that the key fortress of Antonia— so vital to the maintenance of order and the subjugation of the city in case of revolt—was vacated by the Romans and entrusted to the Jewish guard is one which does not commend itself very easily to a thoughtful mind.

The castle was essentially a *barracks*, more suited to occupation by rough soldiery than any other building in Jerusalem. The alternative from the Roman standpoint was Herod's Palace on the south-west hill, which, by reason of its sumptuous apartments and its broad ornamental gardens, was ill-suited to the quartering of troops. When I asked Dr. Sukenik where he thought

Pilate and his wife had their private apartments, he favoured Herod's Palace, on the ground that the presence of coarse soldiers and the noise and stench inseparable from a military barracks would be distasteful to Claudia.

Whatever the truth may be about that matter, the suggestion that Pilate was at *Caesarea and had to be fetched hurriedly to crush the insurrection* is not only contrary to tradition, but is palpably opposed to reason and common sense.

As Governor of the province, directly responsible to the Emperor himself, it was in Pilate's personal interests to preserve order at all costs. The task was admittedly difficult, since on three occasions in the year there were vast pilgrimages to Jerusalem to celebrate the Feasts. Not only was every inch of available space occupied in the city itself, but many thousands of pilgrims were compelled to encamp on the surrounding hills. The Roman rule was intensely distasteful to the Jews, and with the populace raised to a high pitch of religious excitement the capital at these periods was potentially as dangerous as a huge powder-magazine. Anything might happen. It was the clear duty of the Governor to be on the spot.

There is not a scintilla of evidence, either in the Gospels or in any other ancient document, that Pilate neglected this duty—*not even in the Slavonic Josephus itself!*

What the Slavonic version says is that "they went and communicated it to Pilate", a perfectly normal proceeding in the circumstances postulated.

There were no telephones in those days, and if something unusual occurred suddenly on the Platform of the Rock—in full view of the garrison of Antonia—the officer of the guard would naturally despatch an urgent courier through the narrow crowded streets of the city to Pilate's apartments in Herod's Palace. The High Priest's house was also in this favoured quarter and Caiaphas, hearing the tumult, or seeing from his windows the scuffle in the Temple Courts below, would almost certainly take steps to inform the Procurator.

This, obviously, is a very different thing from a double deputation, travelling (as Eisler contends) all those stony miles to "distant Caesarea", with a view to bringing Pilate and his legion rather belatedly to the scene.

We begin to see, therefore, that two of Dr. Eisler's basic assumptions are very doubtful "starters".

But the nature of our critic's theory compels him to do something much more drastic and illogical than this. It will be remembered that the major premiss of all this elaborate system of reconstruction and inference is that Pilate's *official report on the case, made within a few days of the Crucifixion, was preserved in the Imperial records at Rome.*

Dr. Eisler quite sincerely believes this to be the fact, and he can, of course, justly claim that both Tertullian and Justin Martyr have left on record statements which seem to imply that they were of a similar opinion. I offer no judgment upon this much-disputed point. It seems to me quite possible that the incident of Jesus did form the subject of a brief entry by the Roman Procurator in the *commentarii* of the Governor at Caesarea from which extracts were regularly sent to the Emperor at Rome.

Eisler, however, goes a step further.

He says that Josephus, finding this document in the *tabularium principis* at Rome, embodied the facts thus disclosed in his first Aramaic draft of the *Jewish War*, thus putting on record the damning circumstances in which Jesus of Nazareth was committed to the Cross. Naturally (he says), the Christians found this "exposure" intolerable and took every step in their power to mutilate and censor the offending passages. Since we owe the preservation of the works of Josephus mainly to the Christians, this would account satisfactorily for the complete silence of the *Jewish War* concerning the tragedy of Christ.

Now I will be perfectly frank with Dr. Eisler.

If he could bring himself to use the rather objectionable phrase *"Christian forger"* with more restraint and with less obvious relish, I, for one, could go a considerable distance with him. I think it is very probable—indeed, almost certain—that there *was* some danger to life, some carrying of secret arms during that fateful Passover by the more fiery and less disciplined of those who supported a new and Messianic régime. I think it is also possible that Josephus did make hostile mention of the case in the Pilate chapter of the *Jewish War* and that the Christians ultimately excised it from their copies. Josephus may even have referred to Jesus as "a malefactor, a rebel, thirsting for kingship".

But I am quite certain that the historian did not extract these details from the Imperial records at Rome,
for this reason:

In order to prove his case, Dr. Eisler cites the well-
known fact that during the Maximinian persecution the
Emperor (Maximinus Daia) caused a document purporting to be the genuine *Acta Pilati* to be "broadcast
in a vast number of copies and listed among the pre-
scribed readings for all the schools of the Empire". We
have the assurance of Eusebius, Bishop of Caesarea, that
such was the case:

> Having forged, to be sure, Memoirs of Pilate and our
> Saviour, full of every kind of blasphemy against Christ, with
> the approval of their chief, they sent them round to every
> part of his dominions, with edicts that they should be ex-
> hibited openly for everyone to see in every place, both town
> and country, and that the primary teachers should give them
> to the children, instead of lessons, for study and committal
> to memory. (*Eccles. Hist.*, IX, 4, 5.)

Now this celebrated document, which these unfortunate children had to learn by heart, had one most awkward
peculiarity. It was dated *A.D. 21*, five years before
Tiberius, at the instance of Sejanus, sent Pilate to Judea.
If the memoirs, therefore, were genuine the Crucifixion
must have taken place in the spring of A.D. 21; yet
Tacitus in his *Annals* (not to mention the Gospels) has
certified for all time that Jesus of Nazareth "suffered
under *Pontius Pilate*".

How does Dr. Eisler meet this very real difficulty?

He does so by adopting A.D. 21 as the true date of the Passion and in order to bring this year within the procuratorship of Pilate he advances the date of Pilate's entry upon his duties to the year A.D. 19, thus giving Pilate a total period of *eighteen* years' residence in Judea instead of ten. We know that Pilate was on his way home when Tiberius died in A.D. 37.

This brings Dr. Eisler into direct and immediate conflict with our standard version of the historian Josephus, who says quite plainly in the *Antiquities* that Vitellius, the Syrian Legate, ordered Pilate home after he had spent *"ten full years"* in Judea. Josephus also says that Valerius Gratus (Pilate's forerunner in office) spent *eleven* years in the province.

Here Eisler does what, to me, is an unconscionable thing. He does not hesitate to accuse "the Christians" of deliberately falsifying the text of Josephus so as "to conceal the true date of the Passion". This, he contends, was perilously easy:

> converting—a trifling change indeed!—the figure sixteen for the number of years of Pilate's administration (*Ant.* XVII, 4, 1) into ten and the corresponding number (four years) for his predecessor Gratus into eleven, thus making Pilate's administration begin in A.D. 26 instead of in A.D. 19.

The note of exclamation after the words "a trifling change indeed" is Dr. Eisler's, not mine.

Now it so happens that at the very time when this persecution was taking place Eusebius was composing his *Ecclesiastical History*. We can picture him sitting in his room at Caesarea, surrounded by his books, penning that immortal work, and perhaps pausing occasionally to look out across the crowded harbour to the sea beyond.

The edict of the Emperor Maximin had only just been issued, so that Eusebius, in his opening chapter, is able to refer to "those who *the other day* published Memoirs against our Saviour". The recency of the Emperor's action is therefore not in doubt.

Eusebius puts his finger at once upon the weak spot in the Memoirs, of which (he says) "the very date noted at the beginning proves the falsity of those who forged them". Strong language, no doubt, though not stronger than that of Dr. Eisler. But Eusebius is not content with mere counter-accusation. He calls in no less an authority than the Jewish historian himself. Read carefully his actual words:

> The same writer [Josephus] tells us in the eighteenth book of the *Antiquities* that in the twelfth year of the reign of Tiberius . . . Pontius Pilate was entrusted with Judea, and that he remained there for *ten entire years*.

So that vital word "*ten*" was in Eusebius's copy of Josephus—as it still is in ours to-day!

What do you make of this very significant fact?

Remember that Josephus had been dead for nearly two hundred years and his great work, the *Antiquities*, was not only in all the great libraries, but many copies were privately held. Eusebius appeals confidently to this celebrated book, not simply because it supports him, but because of its independent authority throughout the learned world.

Dr. Eisler says that the sole reason for this manipulation by the Christians of the text of Josephus "was to obtain a valid argument against the genuineness of the *Acta* published by Maximinus in A.D. 311".

How could the Christians falsify at short notice a book so familiar and widely dispersed as that?

I submit that Eusebius and his friends could no more have tampered with the received text of the *Antiquities*, lying in the contemporary libraries of Alexandria, Athens, Corinth and Rome, than you or I to-day could alter some disliked sentence in Gibbon's *Decline and Fall of the Roman Empire*. The proposition is plainly indefensible, and not even the schoolchildren of the Graeco-Roman world could have been induced to believe it.

44. STREET OF ARCHES
A typical scene within the City walls

45. THE SO-CALLED TOWER OF DAVID

Built upon Herodian foundations. An impressive reminder of the strength of the fortifications

CHAPTER XIII

REVOLUTION OR SACRIFICE?

WE climbed laboriously back, up the stony and winding path, to the point near the House of Caiaphas where we had left the Hillman.

Lusho unlocked the car and made as though to admit me to my accustomed place, when I took him aside and explained that I wanted him to drive alone to the Garden of Gethsemane, where I would join him at the earliest possible moment. The journey would take him round three sides of the city, past the Damascus and Herod's gates to the point where the Jericho road dives steeply into the upper part of the Kidron valley. From here he would descend and cross a bridge from which a superb view is obtained of the Garden, with its chaste basilica of white stone facing the main road.

From the corner of the city wall, above the Sultan's Pool, I watched the tail of the car disappear, past a blaze of oranges, towards the Jaffa Gate. Then I walked slowly back along the narrow thoroughfare which separates the south wall from the Cenacle and the Church of the Dormition. Immediately opposite the Sion Gate I stood still and took out my watch. The time was exactly eighteen minutes to twelve.

Then walking deliberately at a slow pace—as though conversing with a friend—I traversed the well-worn track which descends to the Kidron valley by a route still high upon the hillside but far below the frowning bastion of the great south-east corner of the wall. I know of no aspect of the city which symbolizes more grimly the ancient strength and grandeur of the fortress of Jerusalem. In early times the bed of the Kidron was from fifty to sixty feet below its present level. It was easy to think of Josephus looking with astonishment (as he describes) over the battlements to the giddy depths below.

As I stumbled painfully down the hillside a man and two oxen were ploughing a field—a picture which has changed little in all these thousand years. Then, rounding the shoulder, the landscape opened and the immortal Garden, in all its quiet and sunny peace, came into view.

Crossing the gully, through which in winter the storm water flows, a hatless figure was coming towards me. It was Lusho Fath'ullah. A smile of joy and relief was on his face. He did not approve of that unattended walk across the lonely slopes of Ophel.

We climbed out of the valley together on to the Bethany road and in a few paces came to Gethsemane. Lusho, with his accustomed thoughtfulness, had parked the car unobtrusively in the shadow of a wall through which an iron gate leads to the Franciscan quarters. A few yards away was the Tree of Agony. I took out my watch. It wanted half a minute to twelve.

It had taken me seventeen and a half minutes to cover the distance traversed by Jesus of Nazareth and His eleven disciples on the night of the Betrayal.

Often in London, sitting in my study, I had longed to make the memorable journey which I have just described—to make it *alone*, without even a companion to share my thoughts. And now I had done it, and the predominant thought in my mind was that the time occupied was seventeen and a half minutes!

Why this insistence upon what, at first sight, would seem to be the *least* relevant of all the moving aspects of that night walk from the Upper Room in Jerusalem to the Garden of the Betrayal? It is a rather long story, but if the reader will bear with me I will try to tell it here.

Many years ago, when I first began seriously to study the tragedy of Jesus, it came home to me with overwhelming force that the key to the mystery lay in a very careful note of the *passage of time*. In any case it was an unprecedented thing for a man, "wanted" by the authorities and with (so to say) a price upon his head, to go voluntarily to a secret rendezvous and wait patiently for the coming of his enemies. Yet this, according to the four Gospels, is precisely what Jesus did and the problem before us is to extract from the rather scanty records some intelligible idea of the secret motives, the by-play of fate and circumstance, which produced this extraordinary result.

Now we can safely assume that the meal which Jesus so greatly desired to take with his followers—for Him, the last meal on earth—would begin about sunset and, having regard to all which is described as taking place, was probably over by eight p.m.—say eight-thirty at the very latest.

Midway in this period one of the little party—Judas Iscariot—finding a valid excuse in the personal needs of the group, of which he was treasurer—leaves the table and goes out into the night. The time of that departure cannot accurately be assessed, but we shall probably not be far wrong if we put it in the neighbourhood of seven to seven-thirty.

At the conclusion of the meal, after the customary singing of the *Hallel*, Jesus and His companions (now reduced to eleven persons) leave the Upper Room and cross unobtrusively to the Garden of Gethsemane—a familiar haunt of Jesus and one which He greatly loved. Allowing for a slight detour, due to the different con-figuration of the ancient city, this journey would prob-ably not occupy more than twenty-five minutes. The party would thus reach the rendezvous not later, say, than nine o'clock.

Then follows a wait of several *hours*, for which we have the very high authority of St. Mark's Gospel, which at this stage seems to be transmitting the account of an eye-witness:

> And they come unto a place which was named Gethsemane and he saith unto his disciples, Sit ye here while I pray. And

180

he taketh with him Peter and James and John. . . . And he went forward a little and fell upon the ground and prayed. . . . And he cometh and findeth them sleeping and saith unto Peter, Simon, sleepest thou? Couldest thou not watch one hour? . . . And he went away again and prayed. . . . And again he came and found them sleeping for their eyes were very heavy. . . . And he cometh the *third* time and saith unto them, Sleep on now and take your rest; it is enough. (Mark xiv, 32–41.)

Note especially those three successive periods of slumber of which the first alone, according to the narrative, lasted *one hour*.

Strong men, wrought to a high pitch of excitement or despair, do not quickly fall asleep. There would necessarily be long periods of anxious watching. Yet St. Mark's testimony in this connection is quite definite. Even the most intimate companions of Jesus fell asleep from sheer weariness not once only, but three times. Throughout this tense, vivid etching of a scene which must have been engraved indelibly upon the minds of those who took part in it, there runs the suggestion of prolonged and patient waiting for something which did not happen quickly— something indeed which was inexplicably delayed. We can hardly postulate a lapse of less than two hours from the time of the arrival in the Garden of Gethsemane to the moment when the glow of torches, illuminating the darkness, announced that the traitor, Judas, was on his way.

Then suddenly, the pace of the drama quickens.

Jesus returns for the fourth time from His solitary com-

181

muning beneath the trees and this time there is a note of urgency in His voice.

I remember as a young man wondering whether from the depths of the Garden it was possible to see clearly a body of men emerging from the city gate. Standing there among the gnarled and ancient trees, on the sloping side of Olivet, my question was answered.

Could you miss them?

Vast as the landscape is, that steep mount, crowned by its frowning battlements, stands out as clearly from every viewpoint as the eastern face of the Matterhorn from Staffel or Hornli. One felt that a strong arm could almost have thrown a stone from the high wall to the precincts of the Garden.

I pictured night falling upon that memorable scene, the long hours of waiting, and, towards midnight, a distant burst of flame as the gates suddenly opened and the arrest-party, with torches held aloft, emerged and moved slowly down the opposing hill, a sinuous trail of fire. And then a quiet voice at my side spoke in accents of decision:

Arise, let us be going: behold he that betrayeth me is *at hand!*

Do you begin to feel the grip of that Marcan narrative? If so, it is a sure sign that at last we are on the track of reality.

Now this formidable gap of time, this tense waiting for something inexplicably delayed, has to be accounted for, and there are numerous hints in the Scriptures which help us to fill in the details. Let us return to that earlier crisis in the story when Judas Iscariot, suddenly rising from the table, left the Upper Room.

St. John alone describes the incident, though it is of course implied by the other Gospels. But the writer of the Fourth Gospel has a habit of giving little personal touches which are very illuminating and he makes it clear that the majority of those present did not see anything in the departure of Judas Iscariot to arouse suspicion.

We can only conjecture what happened, but as keeper of the purse Judas appears to have acted in a corporate capacity for the little band, and it is possible that he openly offered as his excuse the necessity for making certain arrangements which were normally entrusted to him. It seems to me quite certain, however, that the general understanding was that *he would rejoin them in the Garden of Gethsemane.* That restful and secluded retreat was a peculiarly suitable rendezvous, since it stood at the fork of the two roads over the Mount of Olives.

This very plausible excuse clearly did not deceive Jesus. He had long observed a streak in the character of Judas, a fatal flaw which would crack under appropriate pressure, and that pressure was now being applied.

Three nights earlier, during a meal at the house of Simon the leper, Jesus had administered to him a sharp rebuke and with those stern words ringing in his ears this man with a "streak" had paid a furtive visit to the priests. The full purport of that secret conference has not been recorded but St. Mark tells us that:

They promised to give him money. And he sought how he might *conveniently* deliver him unto them.

Note carefully that word "convenient". It is peculiar to St. Mark.

At first sight no doubt it will seem a very extraordinary thing that the Jewish authorities should have been prepared to pay good money to an obscure provincial for facilitating the arrest of an apparently defenceless man, and one who, quite obviously, was not taking any special pains to conceal his whereabouts. The truth is that Jesus was not "defenceless". Indeed, He held just then in His hands a power greater than that wielded by Caiaphas or even by Pontius Pilate himself, and the fulcrum of that potential weapon was the Messianic expectation of the people.

He had only to lift His finger to raise that dense congregation of pilgrims to an unexampled pitch of frenzy and excitement.

It is not merely that, with His unique mental and spiritual equipment, His profound insight into human character, and His devastating power of confounding His opponents, Jesus appeared to many of His contemporaries as the fulfilment of the ancient prophecies. The truth, surely, lies deeper. He *was* the fulfilment of prophecy. Can any one to-day—contemplating all that uneasy dreaming which fills the pages of the Old Testament—seriously doubt that what was troubling those early seers was a prevision of the glory which breaks forth in the teaching of Christ?

And here was that very man—*in Jerusalem*—surrounded by a powder magazine which needed only a spark to cause its detonation. Need we wonder that the authorities hesitated to apply the torch! No one could have foreseen the consequences had Jesus publicly given the word which would have set Him, temporarily at least, on the throne of David. Hence the supreme importance of securing Him *by night* and in circumstances which would preclude the swift circulation of the news in Jerusalem. To have made the arrest in Bethany (even under cover of darkness) would have been highly dangerous. Many thousands of pilgrims were encamped upon the hills and that three-mile march along the Bethany road might well have precipitated the feared detonation.

Indeed there seems to have been quite a strong body of opinion in priestly circles against putting the issue to the test at this particular juncture, since St. Mark says that they

> sought how they might take him *with subtilty* . . . but not during the Feast, lest haply there should be a tumult of the people.

Politically, therefore, the situation was one of peculiar difficulty and it would seem that the essence of the arrangement which Judas made with the priests was that he should keep his eyes open and warn them immediately of any development favourable to their design.

I think it is very probable that when Judas Iscariot entered the Upper Room he had no thought of immediate

action. For the time being he would stick to his job. He
may even have hoped that at the last moment Jesus would
place himself openly at the head of the Messianic movement. The meal had not proceeded very far, however,
before a new and deeply significant fact penetrated his
alert mind. The mood of his leader was sad and very
earnest. He was talking of death—His own death—as
something now inevitable.

What had happened?

Something which the traitor, with his rather cramped
mental and spiritual make-up, could not understand.
Jesus had come to the greatest, the most tremendous
decision of His life. And the tragic thing is that to a mind
of His calibre, to a spirit so loyal to the deeper and
eternal values of human life there was *no alternative*.

Forgive me if I write here with great frankness.

I believe—as, indeed, every sincere student of the
Gospels must believe—that Jesus was fully conscious
that He was, in His own person, the fulfilment of prophecy; that a vision of God had been vouchsafed to Him
which transcended all other visions; and that if ever a
man was justified in claiming to ascend that unique
throne, it was He.

If He could have had it on His own terms, the Messiahship would have been the supreme consummation of His
great and inspired life. There was a time when He seems
to have thought that the two incompatibles, the political
and the spiritual, could be joined. But the events of those
last moving days had brought Him face to face with an

186

inexorable fact. The spiritual Messiahship, which He already held in His own moral right, could not be implemented apart from the political—and that meant *war, bloodshed, a mighty uprising of the Jewish people*, with the certain intervention of the power and the might of Rome.

Consciously, deliberately and with a full sense of the frustration it involved. He set it aside. He chose to be loyal to Himself, to His message, to God and to all that splendid vision which it had been His joy to teach. He chose Death—and this Supper was to tell the disciples that!

As the recital proceeded consternation and despair was written on the faces of His followers but in one a scowl of anger mounted. This was "selling the pass" just when triumph seemed assured. Jesus leaned forward and said quietly to that man:

What thou doest, do quickly!

Judas, obeying the instruction, but in a different sense to that conceived by his companions, rose to his feet and went out into the night.

Here and there some sceptical reader will doubtless protest that no ordinary person would behave in real life as Jesus did that night. We may accept the implied distinction, but I submit to the reader that the more closely we study the historical situation, as portrayed in the Gospels, the clearer it becomes that there is really no escape from the sacrificial view.

187

For nearly two thousand years all sorts and conditions of men have studied the very remarkable teaching contained in the Synoptic Gospels and this has crystallized to-day into something which we call the "Mind of Christ". Project that to the point of the historical dilemma which we are now contemplating, and what do you get? Certainly no bloodstained warrior, "thirsting to be King"!

Indeed, the idea that you can have one kind of Jesus for the purposes of the Crucifixion and another kind of Jesus for the enunciation of the Teaching is absurd. Yet this fallacy lies at the root of most of the attempts to fit a revolutionary Jesus into the framework of fact created by the Christ of the Gospels, and it is this framework with which we are here concerned.

The news, therefore, which Judas was able to convey to Caiaphas was of a very sensational kind. It consisted of two explicit assurances: *first* that the decision of Jesus had been taken and that His mind was already bending to the Cross; *second*, that He would wait conveniently in the Garden of Gethsemane until he (Judas) came. It was a tacit invitation from the "leader" of the feared revolt to pass sentence of death. The information came, however, at a highly inconvenient moment—and there are, of course, still those three hours of tense drama to account for. How were they occupied?

I believe that they can be accounted for, quite adequately, on two basic suppositions. In the first place the decision to arrest Jesus, on the very eve of the Feast, could only have been taken after prolonged discussion between the leaders of the Great Sanhedrin. Certain very grave dangers attended this step, particularly if the strict observance of the Mosaic Law compelled them to hold Jesus until after the celebrations. The repercussion might have been such as to overthrow the hierarchy. It was necessary, therefore, to find some legal formula by means of which the Prisoner could be tried overnight and executed the next morning.

Secondly, the carrying out of this plan was clearly dependent upon the willingness of Pilate to ratify the sentence and give effect to it at short notice. This involved telling him something about the case in advance and ascertaining his reactions to it. Probably the High Priest alone could undertake so delicate a mission and it was doubtless Caiaphas himself who visited the Procurator in his private apartments that night.

This dual necessity, imposed by the peculiar nature of the political and judicial problem confronting the priests, has left its unmistakable mark on the chronology of the Gospels.

It will be recalled that Judas left the Upper Room some time prior to the departure of Jesus for the Garden of Gethsemane. The short journey to the priestly quarter could not have occupied more than five or six minutes. It is reasonable to assume, therefore, that the information which he had to offer would be in the possession of Caiaphas about eight o'clock.

A great deal would have to be done, however, before

the High Priest could be in a position to pay his momentous call upon the Roman Governor. Probably a messenger was sent requesting an audience, but even this vital step could hardly have been taken until some provisional agreement had been reached concerning the *desirability of acting upon this particular night*. We can be reasonably certain that Caiaphas would not have taken the sole responsibility for that decision upon his own shoulders.

We have to think, therefore, of a good deal of coming and going in the Upper City; hurried consultations with the leaders of the dominant parties in the great Sanhedrin; the summoning of the necessary witnesses; the warning of the Temple Guard to be in readiness to effect the arrest.

I cannot personally visualize all this happening within less than two hours, which fixes the time of the interview with Pilate as certainly not earlier than ten o'clock. It may have been much later.

At this period the nature of the "conviction" could not, of course, be known. It was the duty of the *witnesses* to formulate the charge and to bring the accused man before the Court. There were many safeguards in the judicial system to ensure a fair trial, and until the case had actually been heard it was impossible to predict with certainty the particular category into which the conviction would fall. The slightest divergence between the testimony destroyed its validity.

It is thus safe to assume that when Caiaphas did at last present himself at the Royal Palace and was ushered into the presence of Pontius Pilate, he would confine himself to the broader aspects of the problem.

A dangerous revolutionary was at large and was indeed at that moment in the neighbourhood of Jerusalem itself. There had been trouble with this man only two days earlier when, in the course of a violent denunciation of the authorities, he had overthrown the tables of the money-changers in the Temple Courts. It was common knowledge, moreover, that many of the pilgrims were secretly carrying arms, and it was feared that this man —taking advantage of the preoccupation of the loyal public with the preparation for the Feast—might lead an armed revolt. Information had reached them of a place where he could be taken quietly. He would be arrested and tried that night. Would Pilate ratify and execute the sentence the next morning?

All this plainly called for some discussion, because the High Priest was obviously contemplating a *death sentence* —and it was precisely that sort of vindictive sentence that Pilate was there to watch. He could not consistently crucify a Jew for an offence which the Roman law did not recognize as justifying the supreme penalty.

When Caiaphas ultimately left the Palace to set in motion the rather cumbrous machinery of the Jewish State, the matter was probably left open. If the trial resulted in a conviction Pilate would hear the case early the next morning and decide accordingly.

It would appear, therefore, that it must have been nearly midnight when a hastily organized contingent of the Temple Guard—armed with swords and staves, and accompanied by the necessary "witnesses"—moved through the silent streets to the city gate.

The rest we know.

In the flickering light of the torches under those dark trees, the arrest was made. It would have been fatal to have taken the *wrong man* and Judas solved that difficulty by his last, damnable act of treachery—the giving of a kiss. There was a brief show of resistance by the impulsive Peter, but his Master restrained him. To His captors, Jesus uttered a sharp reproach:

> Are ye come out, as against a robber, with swords and staves to seize me. I was daily with you in the Temple teaching and ye took me not, but this is done that the scriptures might be fulfilled.

"That the *scriptures* might be fulfilled!"

It is almost impious to suggest what was then passing in the mind of Jesus, but I fancy that He must have been fortified during that terrible experience by a passage from the Old Testament which He probably knew by heart and upon which in those last crucial hours He plainly moulded his conduct.

We sometimes forget, I think, that the words of Isaiah's noble tribute to the Suffering Servant of God were as *familiar to Jesus* as they are to us. You remember that it opens in a mood of intense sadness. The "suffering servant" is despised and rejected of men, a man of sorrows and acquainted with grief. . . . He is brought as a lamb to the slaughter, and as a sheep before her shearers is

46. THE GARDEN OF GETHSEMANE

Showing the Basilica and the road to Bethany across the foot of Olivet

47. THE "TREE OF AGONY"

Monk picking olives in a corner of the Garden of Gethsemane

dumb so he opened not his mouth. . . . They make his grave with the wicked and with the rich in his death, although he has done no violence, neither has any deceit been found in his mouth.

But the passage concludes upon a note of triumph:

> Therefore will I divide him a portion with the great and he shall divide the spoil with the strong, because *he hath poured out his soul unto death*; he was numbered with the transgressors, and he bare the sins of many and made intercession for the transgressors.

Why should we be troubled by the almost startling alignment of some of these phrases with that larger framework of fact of which I have spoken? Of what import were even the terrors of the Crucifixion in the supreme hour of the conscious fulfilment of a prophecy like that?

I have discussed the Jewish Trial at some length in my book *Who Moved the Stone?* and do not propose to retell the melancholy story here. The proceedings were admittedly illegal. A "trial for life" could not be heard at night; only trials for money could be conducted after sunset. But the Marcan account of these proceedings makes two things abundantly clear:

First. The earlier "witnesses" heard by the Court failed to establish their point. The testimony "agreed not together" and the charge was therefore overthrown.

Second. A further charge was then produced, obviously based upon some statement publicly made by Jesus in the Temple precincts. In this case the witnesses were in substantial agreement, and the charge clearly had weight with the tribunal. The offence alleged was "sorcery" and the

N   193

penalty, under the Jewish system of jurisprudence, death by stoning.

Unfortunately for the Jewish authorities, it was not so regarded by the Roman Law. There were many such disparities between the two legal systems, and, by the direct order of Tiberius, the power to *give effect* to a death sentence had been expressly removed from Jewish hands. The whole case was thus plainly on the point of breaking down when Caiaphas, throwing all pretence of legality to the winds, rose in his seat and applied to the Prisoner the dreaded Oath of the Covenant, to which even silence itself was an unforgivable offence.

I adjure thee by the living God. Art thou the Christ?

It was flagrantly illegal, but Jesus had no alternative but to reply, and He did so at once, plainly and without equivocation: "Thou hast said." This was the traditional form of reply to a question of grave and sad import. Courtesy forbade a direct "Yes" or "No". As Mr. Baring Gould has pointed out, many similar instances will be found in the Talmud.

This unexpected confession gave Caiaphas the material for a far more deadly charge than he had hoped to obtain —the charge of *treason* against the might and majesty of Rome. Pilate would know how to deal with that!

Dramatically rending his garments, as he swung round to his fellow judges, he exclaimed triumphantly: "What need have we of further witnesses?"

The next morning, at a hurried sitting of the Great

Sanhedrin, the sentence was confirmed, though St. Luke tells us that at least one member did not consent to their counsel and deed. Jesus was then dragged to the bar of the Roman Procurator.

Here the writer of St. Matthew's Gospel lifts a corner of the curtain upon an otherwise unreported incident in the domestic affairs of the Roman Governor. He tells us that Claudia, who had accompanied her husband to Jerusalem, *dreamed about the Jewish prisoner that night* and that awakening early the next morning and finding Pilate already gone to his appointment, she sent him an urgent message:

> Have thou nothing to do with that righteous man for I have suffered many things this day in a dream because of him.

Now we may admit at once that this vivid interlude only appears in a single Gospel and is not recorded in the Gospel according to St. Mark. But then St. Mark's terse style causes him to omit many things which, by common consent, are historically true of Jesus. What should we have known, for example, of the magnificent tribute to his kinsman, John the Baptist; or of the Sermon on the Mount; or of such typically Christian parables as those of the Talents, the Marriage Feast, the Unmerciful Servant and the Ten Virgins; or indeed of that supreme classic of devotion, *the Lord's Prayer*, if St. Matthew and St. Luke had not preserved them for us? No one Gospel tells us the whole story. The human mind is highly selective and one individual will recall certain things very vividly, while another remembers something quite different.

I am very reluctant to dismiss St. Matthew's statement as purely legendary for two reasons: in the first place, it is essentially reasonable and true to normal human experience. Secondly, it seems to be required by the peculiar drift of events as described in the other Gospels.

It will be obvious, I think, to any one who seriously considers this question that Claudia was either present at the interview with Caiaphas, or was left to her own resources for a considerable period at a time in the late evening when she had every right to expect her husband's company.

Try to picture the scene.

Pilate and Claudia are in Jerusalem for the Feast and are lodged in Herod's Palace. They could have had few friends in the capital and would thus be thrown much upon each other's company. Midway in the evening a messenger arrives from the High Priest, presenting his apologies for intrusion at such a late hour, but requesting an interview upon an urgent matter of State. After considerable delay this dignitary arrives and is conducted courteously into the Imperial apartments.

The prevailing custom on such occasions may, of course, have necessitated the withdrawal of Claudia to another room. In that case, for many anxious minutes, Pilate would remain closeted with the supreme representative of the Jewish State. So unexpected a break in the social amenities of the Palace—and at such a late hour—could hardly have taken place without Claudia wanting to know all about it. Her husband's destiny was in a sense linked with his successful handling of this very subtle and haughty leader of the Jewish people. A matter so grave as to necessitate this nocturnal meeting was equally grave from her husband's point of view. Claudia would be deeply concerned to know what it portended, and Pilate would have to tell her. After all, she was a daughter (though illegitimate) of the Imperial house.

So much stands clear out of the picture.

But there is another fact which the critical student must not overlook. When Caiaphas left the Palace that night *he put in motion the machinery of the Jewish State*. What does that imply? It implies surely that, despite the uncertainty attaching to the preliminary hearing, the High Priest was reasonably satisfied that (for an adequate offence) Pilate would crucify. Had there been any real doubt on that score Caiaphas and his colleagues would probably have held their hand.

Roughly, therefore, the position is this: Pilate was loosely pledged to carry out the wishes of Caiaphas, providing he was satisfied that the offence justified the penalty. He was probably indifferent to the result, but when the Procurator and his wife retired to rest that night Claudia knew that even then a man was being tried for his life and that her husband would probably execute him the next morning.

Now there was doubtless a time in the progress of

human thought when it was considered necessary to postulate here the existence of some prior acquaintance-ship (or at least close personal sympathy) between Claudia and Jesus to justify the assumption that she dreamed of Him that night. Many scholars have rejected the passage on the ground that the social disparity be-tween the wife of the Roman Governor and an obscure Galilean was such as to render the story very improbable. I submit, however, that recent scientific speculation, par-ticularly in the field of time-physics, has gone far to des-troy the validity of the argument.

Do women *never* have dreams? Do dreams, particularly those of this very vivid sort, *never* come true? Is it not the teaching of the newer philosophy of Time—of which Mr. J. W. Dunne is so brilliant an exponent—that most dreams are compounded of past and *future* experience. Often it is the future experience which produces the most distressing dreams, as when a mother or a wife goes through prematurely the mental agonies of a disaster imminent to one they love.[1]

By all means let us apply our critical faculties to the discussion of the Gospels, but let us at least be sure that we are not resting our criticism upon a shallow and materialistic concept of the Universe which many able

[1] Canon F. W. Green, in his admirable commentary on St. Matthew's Gospel, reminds us that the historian Appian relates a story that Calpurnia, wife of Julius Caesar, had a terrifying dream before his death, on the strength of which she implored him not to proceed to the Forum. A fuller discussion of the contemporary philosophy of time, with special reference to Claudia's dream and the predictions of Jesus, will be found in the Postscript, see pages 259-62.

thinkers already believe to be out-dated and out-worn.

We do not *need the prior knowledge of Claudia*; we need only the awful Fact of the following afternoon and all the misery it was to bring subsequently to herself and her husband.

There is, however, as it seems to me, an even stronger reason for regarding the dream as historic and the evidence lies in the very curious and, in a sense unexpected, turn which events took the following morning.

St. Matthew says quite explicitly that Claudia's message reached Pilate while he was actually "sitting upon the judgment seat". This can only mean that the Procurator had left his private apartments for the scene of the investigation before Claudia awakened. The statement, however, clearly implies something else, viz. that Claudia had grave reasons to fear that her husband was intending formally to ratify the Jewish finding and commit the prisoner (without full and adequate trial) to the Cross!

I see no logical escape from this inference.

If Caiaphas had not obtained reasonable assurances from Pilate overnight, the priests would never have risked the arrest so close to the Feast. If Claudia had not feared this very thing she would never have indited her note in such haste. The two facts fit together in a highly significant way and *they explain the sequel*; for the result was a transient phase in the life of Pontius Pilate which is not only creditable to him, but which provides the one bright spot in all that tragic story.

It is clear from the records that Caiaphas and his friends came to the tribunal of Pilate *without witnesses* and with no formal or prepared plan for the prosecution. They were plainly taken by surprise when the Procurator indicated by his opening sentence that he was going to *rehear the case*:

What accusation bring ye against this man?

This was the *interrogatio*, the formal opening of a Roman trial. Astounded by the sudden change of front they retorted sullenly:

If he were not an evil-doer we would not have delivered him up to thee.

After some further interchange of argument the priests, seeing that Pilate was determined, began to accuse Jesus, saying:

We found this man perverting our nation, and forbidding to give tribute to Caesar, and saying that he himself is Christ a king.

At the mention of the word "king" the Procurator's interest was aroused. This thing clearly called for closer investigation and he took Jesus inside the Praetorium to interview Him privately. What then happened can best be left to the imagination, but the quiet bearing of the Prisoner, His sincere protestation that His "kingdom" was "not of this world" plainly impressed Pilate, and when they again emerged he declared in the most unequivocal fashion the innocence of Jesus:

What evil hath he done? (Mark xv. 14.)
I find no fault in him. (John xviii. 38.)

It is unfortunate from a purely historical standpoint that a fuller and more detailed account of these memorable proceedings has not come down to us. It is quite impossible, however, to study the accounts given in the four Gospels—with all their divergencies and confused recollections of those terrible hours—without realizing that Pilate must have exerted his utmost efforts to get Jesus released.

We see it in the twice declared conviction of innocence, in the reported remission to Herod, in the last desperate offer of Barabbas, and in that final scene when the Procurator, unable any longer to make himself heard above the tumult, symbolically washed his hands of the whole matter.

By this time the space surrounding the tribunal was in an uproar and above the shouting of the crowd came the sharp tones of an authoritative voice:

If thou lettest this man go, thou art not Caesar's friend.

It was an open threat to carry the issue to Vitellius, the legate of Syria, and Pilate knew it. The barbed shaft went home. Weakly he gave way. And as the din rose to pandemonium around Jesus and His accusers another sound was heard echoing through the corridors of the Praetorium. It was the dreaded order, called out sharply by the officer of the Roman Guard: *Ite Tenete Eum*— "Go, Hold Him!"

CHAPTER XIV

TRACING AN ANCIENT STORY BACKWARDS

IT was the Roman custom for the centurion in charge of a crucifixion to nail a *"titulus"* or superscription to the cross of the condemned man and the Gospels are agreed that, in the case of Jesus of Nazareth, this bore the brief, but obviously ironic description: "The King of the Jews".

The writer of the Fourth Gospel, however, reports an additional fact of considerable interest. He tells us that the priests resented the implication and approached Pilate with a view to having the wording altered. They wanted to make it quite clear to the onlookers that the claim to the royal title had no sort of official backing and that the great mass of the loyal public was not associated with it.

Technically, of course, the suggestion was a perfectly reasonable one. Irony had no place in a bald official document, and the *titulus* as it then stood implied more than an isolated and unsuccessful attempt to seize the civil power. It implied disloyalty and treason towards the Emperor on the part of the whole nation. The priests desired Pilate to substitute for these damaging words the more precise statement: "He *called himself* the King of the Jews".

I quite agree with Dr. Eisler that this episode is almost certainly historic:

> It is obvious that the designation of a hanged person as "King of the Jews" must have been regarded as an insult to the whole Jewish people. . . . The Sanhedrin must therefore inevitably have expostulated to Pilate that he should alter the title indicating the cause of punishment. (Page 514.)

The appeal was apparently unsuccessful.

Pilate was in a testy and impatient mood. He had clearly been forced to take punitive action against his will, and he would not budge an inch. "What I have written, I have written." They must take it or leave it.

Later in the afternoon, however, when the awful scene on Calvary had already reached its close, an incident occurred which shows Pilate in a more normal and reasonable frame of mind, and here, it should be noted, we have the *whole weight of the Gospel tradition behind us.*

It is rather confidently asserted by some critics, to whom the New Testament writings are generally suspect, that in all human probability the body of Jesus of Nazareth was thrown into the common pit. Such was the fate of felons, and I am inclined to agree that in normal circumstances this might have happened in the present case.

But the circumstances surrounding this tragedy were not normal.

It is clear that the Procurator committed Jesus to the Cross very much against his better judgment and under strong personal and political pressure from the High Priest. There was, without doubt, some support for the spiritual claims of Jesus even in the Great Sanhedrin itself. Outside that body there were thousands who were ready to do Him honour and who were profoundly distressed and shocked at the unexpected course which events had taken. "We hoped that it was he who should redeem Israel." (Luke xxix, 21.)

It would not be surprising, therefore, if some stray passage had reached us to the effect that, in death, He had been given an honourable burial.

The literary evidence, however, is much more definite and explicit, because all the Gospels assure us that, shortly after the Crucifixion, a certain man went to Pontius Pilate and sought permission to bury the body. St. Mark, to whose version special authority attaches in respect of the Jerusalem tradition, says that:

> when even was come (because it was the Preparation, that is, the day before the Sabbath) there came Joseph of Arimathea, a councillor of honourable estate who also himself was looking for the Kingdom of God; and he went boldly in unto Pilate and asked for the body of Jesus.

St. Mark also records a fact, which is not expressly mentioned by the other writers, but which I see no reason to regard as other than historic. He says that "Pilate marvelled if he were *already* dead: and calling unto him the centurion he asked him if he had been any while dead. And when he learned it of the centurion he granted the corpse to Joseph".

Now Dr. Kirsopp Lake, in his very interesting discussion of the Resurrection narratives, makes some play with the fact that the Gospels are not agreed concerning the *status* of Joseph.

St. Matthew describes him as "a rich man from Arimathea who also himself was Jesus' disciple". St. Luke, who repeats the Marcan statement that Joseph was "a councillor looking for the Kingdom of God" adds that he was a good man and righteous and that "he had not consented to their counsel and deed". The writer of St. John's Gospel says that he was "a disciple of Jesus, but secretly for fear of the Jews".

I do not personally see anything in these slightly differing statements to cause critical disquiet. Jointly they succeed quite admirably in conveying the impression of a man of good social position, probably a member of the Sanhedrin, who was secretly sympathetic to the cause of Christ. When the whole episode was closed and his hopes of an earthly consummation shattered, Joseph had the moral courage to come out into the open. Scorning the criticism of his colleagues, he went "*boldly* to Pilate and asked for the body of Jesus".

Whatever the true facts concerning his social or official status may have been, however, the Gospels are in absolute agreement that the name of this man was *Joseph of Arimathea*, that he went to Pilate with this particular request, that Pilate *granted permission*, and that Joseph actually *arranged and conducted the burial.*

I stress these four points of fundamental agreement because, according to St. Matthew, the priests, twenty-four hours later, returned to Pilate with an urgent request that he should set a military guard over the tomb.

This raises an historical issue of the first magnitude, since St. Matthew is the only Evangelist to refer to the episode, and the story of the guard as he relates it is regarded by many scholars as the product of a much later age—a kind of echo of the controversy which raged throughout the early Christian era concerning the tomb of Christ.

I confess that, as a young student, the critical case against the historicity of the incident seemed to me to be of conclusive weight. About ten years ago, however, I had occasion to make a rather close study of the circumstances surrounding the death of Jesus. I was impressed by the deep hold which this story had secured in the apocryphal literature and it occurred to me that it might be profitable to *trace it backwards* to its first primitive mention in the New Testament.

Now there are three classic references to the Story of the Guard in documents of unquestioned antiquity and they appear in the following time sequence:

(*a*) St. Matthew's Gospel, which Harnack dates about the time of the destruction of Jerusalem.

(*b*) The very primitive Gospel of Peter, which clearly embodies much archaic material and which is generally assigned to the early part of the second century.

(*c*) The so-called Gospel of Nicodemus or Acts of Pilate, a document issued in the Christian interest, probably at the beginning of the fourth century, as a counterblast to the alleged disclosures by the Emperor Maximin.

We will take the latest of these versions first.

In the Gospel of Nicodemus we read a great deal about the fury of the priests towards Joseph of Arimathea, whose action in giving Jesus an honourable burial had clearly aroused strong resentment. The details of this controversy do not concern us here, but the passage which follows deals with the story of the guard and is of considerable interest.

> And while they sat in the synagogue and marvelled because of Joseph, there came certain of the guard which the Jews had asked of Pilate to keep the sepulchre of Jesus lest peradventure his disciples should come and steal him away. And they spake and declared unto the rulers of the synagogue and the priests and the Levites that which had come to pass: how that there was a great earthquake, and we saw an angel descend from heaven, and he rolled away the stone from the mouth of the cave, and sat upon it. And he did shine like snow and like lightning, and we were sore afraid and lay as dead men. And we heard the voice of the angel speaking with the women which waited at the sepulchre, saying: Fear ye not: for I know that ye seek Jesus which was crucified. He is not here: he is risen, as he said. Come, see the place where the Lord lay, and go quickly and say unto his disciples that he is risen from the dead and is in Galilee.[1]

[1] I am indebted to the Clarendon Press, Oxford, for permission to quote the relevant extracts from the late Dr. M. R. James's translation of the apocryphal documents referred to in this chapter. *The New Testament Apocrypha,* 1924.

Then comes the following extraordinary conversation:

The Jews say: With what women spake he? They of the guard say: We know not who they were. The Jews say: At what hour was it? They of the guard say: At midnight. The Jews say: And wherefore did ye not take the women? They of the guard say: We were become as dead men through fear, and we looked not to see the light of day; how then could we take them? The Jews say: As the Lord liveth we believe you not. They of the guard say unto the Jews: So many signs saw ye in that man, and ye believed not, how then should ye believe us? Verily ye sware rightly "as the Lord liveth", for he liveth *indeed*. Again they of the guard say: We have heard that ye shut up him that begged the body of Jesus, and that ye sealed the door: and when ye had opened it ye found him not. Give ye therefore Joseph and we will give you Jesus. The Jews say: Joseph is departed unto his own city. They of the guard say unto the Jews: Jesus also is risen, as we have heard of the angel, and he is in Galilee.

The narrative then concludes as follows:

And when the Jews heard these words they were sore afraid, saying: *Take heed* lest this report be heard and all men incline unto Jesus. And the Jews took counsel and laid down much money and gave it to the soldiers, saying: Say ye: While we slept his disciples came by night and stole him away. And if this come to the governor's hearing we will persuade him and secure you. And they took *the money* and did as they were instructed. And this their saying was published abroad among all men.

It is hardly necessary to remind the reader that the references to the *women* in this passage are completely at variance with the much earlier tradition preserved in the New Testament. St. Mark, who was the first to commit

that tradition to writing, says quite explicitly that the
women came to the tomb "very early on the first day
of the week *when the sun was risen*". St. Matthew's phrase
is: "as it *began to dawn* towards the first day of the week".
St. Luke says "*at early dawn*".

The whole weight of the Synoptic tradition is therefore
behind the accepted belief that the women did not reach
the garden before dawn, although they doubtless rose
while it was still dark. Yet in the Gospel of Nicodemus
the women are depicted quite irrationally as watching
at the tomb *throughout the night*. It is clear that by the time
this narrative was written the local tradition had deterior-
ated in two vital respects. Pilate was thought of as having
placed a military guard at the tomb and the writer's mind
was extremely confused concerning the part played by
the women in the events of Sunday morning.

So much for the fourth century. Let us now go back
about a hundred and seventy years to that very famous
document, known as the Gospel of Peter. Only a few
fragments remain but the relevant passages read thus:

> And the elders were afraid and came unto Pilate, entreating
> him and saying: Give us soldiers that we [or they] may watch
> his sepulchre for three days, lest his disciples come and steal
> him away and the people suppose that he is risen from the
> dead, and do us hurt. And Pilate gave them Petronius the
> centurion with soldiers to watch the sepulchre; and the elders
> and scribes came with them unto the tomb, and when they
> had rolled a great stone to keep out . . . the centurion and
> the soldiers, then all that were there together set it upon the
> door of the tomb; and plastered thereon seven seals; and they
> pitched a tent there and kept watch.

Here follows a highly imaginative account of the Resurrection itself, upon which, of course, the Gospels are silent. The document then proceeds in a much more sober tone:

> Now early on the Lord's day Mary Magdalene, a disciple of the Lord—which, being afraid because of the Jews, for they were inflamed with anger, had not performed at the sepulchre of the Lord those things which women are accustomed to do unto them that die and are beloved of them—took with her the women her friends and came unto the tomb where he was laid. And they feared lest the Jews should see them, and said: Even if we were not able to weep and lament him on that day whereon he was crucified, yet let us now do so at his tomb. But who will roll away for us the stone also that is set upon the door of the tomb, that we may enter in and sit beside him and perform that which is due? for the stone was great, and we fear lest any man see us. And if we cannot do so, yet let us cast down at the door these things which we bring for a memorial of him, and we will weep and lament until we come unto our house.

The dependence of this Gospel upon the original Marcan tradition is, in certain places, very noticeable, but observe what has happened.

We are now in the early years of the Second Century. Pontius Pilate is still the sponsor of the guard. He calls Petronius the centurion and a few soldiers and places these at the disposal of the priests. But the women are plainly back out of the doubtful region of midnight to the logical and almost certainly historic period of dawn. The whole atmosphere of the passage just quoted suggests that Mary Magdalene and her friends went to the tomb for a specific and quite natural purpose at the earliest opportunity *consistent with the light*. This is a very definite gain. In this respect at least, an air of reality is invading the picture.

Now go back a further fifty or sixty years and read carefully the account of the same incident as it appears in the Gospel according to St. Matthew:

> Now on the morrow, which is the day after the Preparation, the chief priests and the Pharisees were gathered together unto Pilate, saying, Sir, we remember that that deceiver said, while he was yet alive, After three days I rise again. Command therefore that the sepulchre be made sure until the third day, lest haply his disciples come and steal him away, and say unto the people, He is risen from the dead; and the last error will be worse than the first. Pilate said unto them, Ye have a guard: go your way, make it as sure as ye can. So they went, and made the sepulchre sure, sealing the stone, the guard being with them.

Here St. Matthew gives his own characteristic version of the women's visit to the tomb. He then resumes the interrupted narrative:

> Now while they were going, behold, some of the guard came to the city, and told unto the chief priests all the things that were come to pass. And when they were assembled with the elders, and had taken counsel, they gave large money to the soldiers, saying: Say ye, His disciples came by night and stole him away while we slept. And if this come to the Governor's ears, we will persuade him, and rid you of care. So they took the money, and did as they were taught: and this saying was spread abroad among the Jews, and continueth until this day.

The reader has thus before him everything which is

essential to the forming of an independent and impartial judgment upon the historical significance of the story. What conclusions are we to draw from it?

Now we may agree at once, I think, that in these deeply interesting narratives we have what has been called "a fragment of controversy" concerning the implied or asserted emptiness of the tomb of Christ. There can be little doubt that this issue was raised very early in the Christian campaign and it would have been surprising if some traces of the dispute had not descended to us. Fortunately we are able to examine the arguments on both sides over a period of nearly four centuries and it is clear that throughout this long period the main contention of the opponents of Christianity was not (as we should have expected) that the remains of Jesus had never been disturbed and still rested where Joseph had laid them, but that *the disciples had stolen the body.*

The persistence of this statement through successive centuries is impressive. We find it unchanged as late as the time of Eusebius. We find it in the Gospel of Peter. We find it stated with supreme clearness in St. Matthew: "Say ye, His disciples came and stole him away while we slept." That the charge was even then of long standing is shown by the concluding words of the Evangelist: "And this saying was spread abroad among the Jews and *continueth until this day.*"

So grave an accusation could not, of course, be ignored by the Christians and it has been suggested that the story of the guard arose out of the widespread circulation of this grossly untrue, but very damaging statement. Dr. Kirsopp Lake has put the case very lucidly in his book, *The Resurrection of Jesus Christ.*

> Faced by the Christian belief in the Resurrection, and the implied or asserted emptiness of the tomb, the Jews invented the explanation that the disciples had stolen the body. The Christians replied that this could not be, for the Jews themselves had placed a guard at the tomb—some said at once, others on the Sabbath after the burial. The Jews retorted by asking why, if so, the soldiers had not seen the Resurrection; and the Christians replied that they had done so, but had concealed their evidence—some said because they had been bribed by the Jews, others because Pilate had ordered them to do so. Thus the most probable view is that this incident is nothing more than a fragment of controversy, in which each imputed unworthy motives to the other, and stated suggestions as established facts. Any controversy in any age will supply parallels. (Page 180.)

In due course (says Dr. Lake) these controversial statements and counter-statements were dramatized into a story. By the eighth or ninth decade of the first century the legend was fully formed and was embodied in St. Matthew's Gospel. Granted that the story was not true, yet neither was the wicked insinuation it was meant to combat. Unconsciously, diamond was set to cut diamond.

Such, briefly, is the explanation of the incident put forward by many sincere and able students of the Gospels to-day and, as such, it deserves our close attention and respect. *But is it the historical explanation?* I venture to suggest that it is not and that there are very strong textual

213

and other reasons for believing that at the root of this old-world story there lies a germ of historic fact.

In the first place the story as told in St. Matthew's Gospel—the earliest account we possess—differs in one vital respect from that set forth in the later and corrupt versions which we have just considered, since Pontius Pilate, when asked by the priests to guarantee the tomb, *refuses the request*:

Ye have a guard: go your way, make it as secure as ye can.

Thereupon the Jewish leaders—relying exclusively upon the services of the Temple Guard—make their own arrangements for policing the garden.

All this tends to support the historicity of the incident, since the Procurator is represented as acting, not only in a very characteristic, but in a strictly constitutional way. The Crucifixion itself was, of course, a Roman act, and had the body of Jesus been cast into the common pit it would have been the duty of Pilate to see that no commotion arose in respect of it. It must not be forgotten, however, that, at the express request of Joseph of Arimathea—a distinguished and possibly official member of the ruling caste—the remains of Jesus had been released from Roman custody with a view to individual and decent burial. *The matter had therefore passed technically out of Pilate's jurisdiction.* He was probably tired of the whole business, but he was certainly within his rights in insisting that the protection of a private estate was for the Jewish authorities themselves. This was clearly the "correct" procedure in the known circumstances—a point which

214

could hardly be lost upon those who, a few hours earlier, had so pointedly threatened to report him to Caesar.

It is significant also that the *chronology* of St. Matthew's account is peculiar and makes his version of the story palpably, and even ludicrously, unsuited to the apologetic uses to which it is supposed to have been put.

We are asked to think of the placing of the guard as a purely fictitious incident, invented by the Christians as a conclusive disproof of the calumny that they had stolen the body. It said in effect: How could the disciples rifle the tomb if, in fact, the enclosure was guarded? If it did not mean that, it meant nothing. Had the story, therefore, sprung fully fledged—without any historic content whatsoever—out of the apologetic needs of the Christians of a later date it would surely have secured this vital point.

But it is not so.

According to St. Matthew, the priests did not go to Pilate on the day of the Crucifixion, but "*on the morrow, which is the day after the preparation*". St. Mark tells us that Jesus was buried late on Friday afternoon, "when even was come, because it was the preparation, that is, the day before the Sabbath". We are faced, therefore, by the highly significant fact that, according to the earliest extant version of the incident, the tomb of Christ was left unguarded *throughout the whole of the first night of the interment.* Moreover, the guards are reported, on their own declaration to have slept during some part of the few remaining hours which are relevant to the problem.

We are thus confronted with a story, purporting to show the impossibility of the disciples tampering with the tomb, with *two gaping intervals of time* during which they had every opportunity of doing this very thing. A grave unprotected for a whole Sabbath (including one invaluable night) and a guard prone to slumber during what was left of the disputed period are very strange ingredients in a story calculated to convince sceptics that the disciples were physically, as well as morally, incapable of such a deception.

Why was it that, fifty years later, when the story was retold, with many imaginative details, in the Gospel of Peter, Pilate is represented as setting the guard *on the day of the Crucifixion itself?* Was it not to close this very awkward gap, which was too inconvenient to have been invented, but was probably imposed upon the earliest version of the narrative by the course of events themselves?

I submit, therefore, that there is, at least, a strong prima facie case (derived from the very texture of the documents themselves) for believing that the Jewish leaders, doubtless for very good reasons, decided rather belatedly to police the garden.

The delay in reaching this decision is not very difficult to understand. The morning of the Crucifixion, and the night which preceded it, were periods of ceaseless and exhausting activity for Caiaphas and the leaders of the Great Sanhedrin. It is possible that news of what Joseph had done did not reach Annas or Caiaphas until the next morning. On the other hand, they may, quite reasonably, have assumed that suitable arrangements would be made by the Romans for the disposal of the three bodies. The Deuteronomic law forbidding the exposure of corpses after sunset (Deut. xxi, 22, ff.) applied quite as much to the two malefactors as it did to the central figure of the Crucifixion.

Given, therefore, the knowledge that the Governor had specially released the body of Jesus from Roman custody, it must have been realized at once that a situation full of disquieting possibilities had arisen. The responsibility for dealing with any disorder at the tomb of the Nazarene was now thrown back upon the shoulders of the priests. The resources of the Temple Guard were, of course, quite inadequate to cope with a major disturbance of the peace and it is, I think, strictly within the realm of historic probability to assume that the Jewish leaders— faced by a possible rallying of the disaffected elements at the tomb of their erstwhile leader—did approach Pilate in this sense.

The force of this argument came home to me very strongly during the course of my stay in Palestine.

Sitting in London or New York, with only the Gospels before us, it is comparatively easy to think of Joseph of Arimathea reverently burying the body of Jesus while the whole dynamic mass of excited pilgrims continued quietly with their preparations for the Feast! Believe me, you cannot feel like that in Jerusalem itself.

I am reluctant to raise here the much-debated question as to whether the Holy Sites uncovered by Queen Helena in the year A.D. 326 were the authentic scene of these memorable events. I am content to leave that an open issue pending further discoveries along the line of the ancient wall. But if the present Church of the Holy Sepulchre—so close to the battlements and to the Gate Gennath—really does stand upon the original site of Calvary, then I am perfectly sure that *some kind of protection* for Joseph's garden was inevitable.

The Roman historian Tacitus tells us that the normal population of Jerusalem was 600,000, but according to Josephus this rose periodically to seven figures, particularly during the Passover. Accommodation was lacking for such a vast influx of pilgrims, and many thousands of these were accustomed to encamp upon the surrounding hills. It is known that at this particular Festival feelings were running high and it seems to me very unlikely that the grave of the victim of so sensational a trial—*lying conveniently within two minutes' walk of the city gate*—should have been left wholly unprotected. We could not do it to-day. It could hardly have been done then. It is, perhaps, not without significance that, in the Gospel of Peter, we read that on Sunday morning "there came a multitude from Jerusalem and the region round about" to see the sepulchre.

Having regard, therefore, to all the circumstances of that tragic week-end, there appear to be very strong indications that the story, as it originally circulated, did not possess the markedly apologetic character which it assumed later.

It seems to me that the action of Joseph of Arimathea,

in according to Jesus the honour of independent burial, must have seriously embarrassed the civil authorities in Jerusalem who were charged with the difficult task of maintaining public decency and order during the Feasts. It threw upon them, at very short notice, the responsibility of policing a small private estate containing the remains of the most notorious of the three prisoners executed the previous afternoon. Many insurgent pilgrims, who had supported the political messiahship of Jesus, were probably among those encamped upon the high ground near the Mamilla pool, in dangerously close proximity to the Gate Gennath and also to the tomb itself. All this suggests the need for special watchfulness at a time when the Temple Guard was fully occupied elsewhere. Hence the fury of the priests against Joseph, which is so strongly reflected in the apocryphal literature.

The fact that (according to St. Matthew) the request to Pilate to relieve them of this responsibility was made on the day *following* the Crucifixion provides textual corroboration of a peculiarly weighty kind. There is no conceivable reason why this highly inconvenient chronology (admitting, as it did, that the tomb was left unguarded for a whole night) should have crept into the story if it did not derive from ineradicable memories of the fact itself.

So much, I think, lies upon the surface of the problem.

The curious thing is, however, that if this possibility is explored further, two considerations emerge which must, I think, give occasion for serious thought to any impartial student of the Gospels. The first concerns the excuse which the priests are reported to have used in their discussion with Pilate.

> Sir, we remember that that deceiver *said*, while he was yet alive, *after three days.* . . .

Let us summon to our aid all the cogent arguments which can be advanced against the historicity of that sentence in the very precise and definitive form in which it is stated by St. Matthew. It clearly attributes to the priests pre-knowledge of the Resurrection. It introduces a tendentious note into an otherwise straightforward narrative. It is the kind of statement which, even if the priestly delegation itself attached importance to it, would have seemed derisory to the mind of the pagan Governor.

And yet when we go right back to the primitive Synoptic account of the trial of Jesus, *conducted by these very priests during the night of the preceding Thursday,* we find, deeply embedded therein as a sort of permanent challenge to our restless and inquiring minds, the fact that the earliest and most protracted phase of that illegal sitting concerned a statement of Jesus embodying those very words: "in three days":

> (*a*) *Witness at the Trial* (*according to St. Mark*)*:* "I will destroy this temple that is made with hands and in three days I will build another made without hands."
>
> (*b*) *Witness at the Trial* (*according to St. Matthew*)*:* "I am able to destroy the temple of God and to build it in three days."
>
> (*c*) *St. John's account of the original saying:* "Destroy this temple and in three days I will raise it up."

Let us grant that the witnesses at the trial perverted, for their own purposes, some statement of Jesus made in a somewhat different context, but the insistence of all the testimonies that the disputed phrase contained those three words is impressive. They were words which could be used appropriately in singularly few connections. Either they were part of a fantastic boast of magical power in relation to the physical Temple—a suggestion uncongenial to our whole tradition about Christ—or they were symbolic of something deeper as suggested by St. John. The reader will form his own conclusions.

It is significant, however, that, in the earliest Gospel (apart from the record of those judicial proceedings), they occur only four times—in the derision at the Cross and in the famous predictions in which Jesus is reported to have foretold His own premature death and ultimate triumph. As I have remarked elsewhere, it is strange that the most challenging phrase in those predictions, which reason asserts could never have been uttered by Jesus, should appear at the very heart and core of the midnight trial before Caiaphas.[1]

The fact must also not be overlooked that the chrono-

[1] That Jesus clearly foresaw the fate which awaited Him at the hands of the Jewish leaders is, I think, generally admitted and, towards the end, He seems to have tried to prepare His followers for that dire event. With His deep sense of the eternal values of human life, He is unlikely to have done this without affirming His unshakable conviction of survival. We are apt to forget that Judas Iscariot was present during these conversations. It is not, therefore, historically precluded that the traitor may have reported to the priests a private statement of Jesus not very dissimilar from that recorded by St. Matthew.

logy of the story, as it is related by St. Matthew, does not conflict in any logical or material aspect with the primitive Marcan tradition of the women's visit to the tomb. Indeed, had such been the case, it could hardly have been introduced with acceptance into St. Matthew's Gospel.

We may agree at once, I think, that had Mary Magdalene and her friends known (late on Saturday afternoon) that the garden was being placed under official surveillance, they would never have planned to perform those last sad rites at the grave of their dead Master. But the evidence is that the garden was *not guarded at the time those plans were made*, and it is very unlikely that a secret decision, reached hurriedly by the authorities only a few hours earlier, should have become known to these Galilean women before they retired (possibly a little earlier than usual) to rest that night.

We must think, therefore, of the women setting out at early dawn, expecting to find the garden deserted and fearing, as they said, lest any man should see them. A few minutes later they are depicted as returning in haste to Jerusalem with their mission unfulfilled. St. Mark says graphically that "they fled from the tomb, for trembling and astonishment had come upon them." St. Matthew describes them as running quickly to inform the disciples.

It is at this point in the Marcan framework that the writer of St. Matthew's Gospel inserts the vital section of the story of the guard. "While they (the women) were going"—he says—*some* of the watch came to the chief priests and reported the things which were come to pass. The word "some" is possibly significant. It suggests that the responsible officers alone reported to the priests, the subordinate members of the watch having presumably returned, either direct to their homes or to their official quarters within the Temple precincts. Thus, the incentive of the women to carry out their self-imposed task is not only logically maintained in the story, but the absence of the guard at the time of its attempted fulfilment is clearly postulated.

If, historically speaking, the problem could be left there, it might reasonably be contended that those responsible for inserting the supposed legend into St. Matthew's Gospel had displayed remarkable ingenuity in adjusting its chronology to the primitive Christian belief concerning the women's visit to the tomb. Obviously, however, it cannot so be left, because right back in the early Marcan account of the events of that memorable dawn, there lie deeply embedded three inferences to which we are bound, in the strictest historical sense, to attach peculiar weight:

First. That the women were *prevented* from carrying out the primary purpose of their surreptitious visit to the garden.

Second. That the gôlal or circular stone, the size of which had caused them considerable anxiety, was *already moved away* from the door of the cave.

Third. That they encountered, *within the tomb,* a young man who actually spoke to them, but the full purport of whose message they did not apparently wait to hear.

Now St. Mark's delineation of the posture of this "young man" is extraordinarily vivid—indeed it is so graphic and precise as to suggest the work of an eye-witness. He describes him as "sitting" in the tomb "on the right side". If the reader will study Eric Matson's striking photograph of the interior of the Garden Tomb at Jerusalem, reproduced in Plate 55, it will convey to him something of the atmosphere required for reconstruction of the scene. It is obviously an abnormal thing for any one to be *sitting* in a tomb at dawn, and the very terse phraseology of St. Mark suggests an attitude of close and absorbed contemplation of the stone ledge upon which the body of Jesus had rested, as though there remained there some visible evidence of its recent occupation.

The Christian believer, who, with the eye of assured faith, identifies the "young man" of St. Mark with the celestial visitants described in the later Gospels will, of course, have no difficulty with this passage. But Dr. Kirsopp Lake, and some other modernists, have argued very forcibly that this reported encounter with a living person at the tomb is an historic necessity, in view of the swift and agitated retirement of the women from the garden. Personally, I feel the weight of that contention very strongly, but surely, *at that exceptionally early hour*, the only way in which any one in Jerusalem could have known that there was something of special interest to see at the tomb of the Nazarene was by the direct report of some one who had just returned from it, and curiously enough, the only body of persons who answer in any effective and human sense to that description is the Guard of the Gospels.

It is, however, clearly outside the scope of this study to discuss the many critical aspects of the Resurrection Narratives. I have dealt with this subject at some length in my book *Who Moved the Stone?* and the interested reader is also referred to the Postscript of the present volume.

CHAPTER XV

THE SAMARITAN AFFAIR

WE have now studied the character of Pilate, under fairly strong illumination, during three typical phases of his official career. The result of this examination is to destroy some ancient prejudices and to reveal the Procurator in a fresh and possibly more human light.

In the earliest episode we found him at Caesarea—fresh to his job as Governor of Judea, and very conscious of his status as the direct representative of Caesar in this comparatively obscure corner of the Roman world. He commits a political blunder of the first magnitude, preferring to assert his newly acquired authority rather than to conform to the wise and far-seeing practice of those who have preceded him. The boomerang returns to his own palace and for some days he obstinately refuses to face the facts. When, at length, these can no longer be denied, he gives way and recognizes, rather belatedly, the strong religious convictions of his subjects.

We must note, however, that on this occasion there was no violence. Had a single Jew perished as a result of the demonstration at Caesarea, Josephus would surely have reported it. The incident must therefore be regarded as a bloodless victory for the common people.

In the second episode we see a maturer and more sophisticated Pilate. He is now deep in his work as an administrator and engineer. The construction of the great aqueduct connecting the Pools of Solomon with the Temple cisterns shows him to be a hard-working, competent and loyal upholder of the Roman tradition. The aqueduct doubtless had a political significance since it assured an adequate reserve of fresh water within the fortifications in the event of a siege. In the course of these operations Pilate compels the Jewish authorities—possibly against their will—to finance the work and, when the populace revolts, he suppresses the riot with firmness and vigour. There are signs throughout this period of a fairly close collaboration with Caiaphas, the High Priest, whom Pilate kept in office throughout the full period of his tenure of the procuratorship.

This brings us to the third and most tragic episode of all—the trial and crucifixion of Jesus of Nazareth. Here the scene is illuminated by strong shafts of light falling upon it from different angles. We have to read a good deal between the lines, but the peculiar character of the political situation enables us to infer some facts with considerable certainty.

For the first time there are signs of a rift between the Roman Procurator and the astute courtier who was the real arbiter of the destinies of Judea. In the preliminary discussions with Caiaphas, prior to the arrest of Jesus,

Pilate seems, quite seriously, to have given the impression that he would endorse the Jewish finding. Yet, when the occasion for ratification arrives, he unexpectedly demurs and uses the whole weight of his influence to secure the release of the prisoner. He misjudges, however, the subtilty of his opponent and, when the dreaded threat is at last launched to report him to Caesar, his resolution fails and one of the gravest miscarriages of human justice is consummated with his unwilling consent.

Such is the picture of this unhappy man as it emerges from the pages of the Jewish historian and of the New Testament.

Only one further brief glimpse of the Roman Procurator is vouchsafed to us and that occurs in the *Antiquities*:

But the nation of the Samaritans did not escape without tumults. The man who excited them to it, was one who thought lying a thing of little consequence, and who contrived everything so that the multitude might be pleased; so he bade them get together upon mount Gerizzim, which is by them looked upon as the most holy of all mountains, and assured them that, when they were come thither, he would show them those sacred vessels which were laid under that place, because Moses put them there. So they came thither armed, and thought the discourse of the man probable; and as they abode at a certain village, which was called Tirathaba, they got the rest together to them, and desired to go up the mountain in a great multitude together; but Pilate prevented their going up, by seizing upon the roads with a great band of horsemen and footmen, who fell upon those that were gotten together in the village; and when it came to an action, some of them they slew, and others of them they put to flight, and took a great many alive, the principal of

48. ROBINSON'S ARCH

The "spring" of a famous arch which once bridged the Tyropean Valley

49. BRIDGE OVER THE TYROPEAN VALLEY

Imaginary reconstruction of the famous viaduct by Mr. E. F. Beaumont

whom, and also the most potentate of those that fled away, Pilate ordered to be slain.

Here again the actual language of Josephus does not seem to justify the flood of vituperation which it has since brought down upon the head of Pilate.

The incident is usually represented as though a perfectly harmless body of peace-loving Samaritans desired simply to ascend their sacred mountain, Gerizim, with the object of searching for relics believed to be concealed beneath the ruins of their Temple, and that Pilate, without any serious provocation, seized this opportunity to put them to the sword. The Temple at Gerizim was once the rival of Jerusalem but was destroyed by Hyrcanus about 110 B.C.

The Samaritans, however, were not a particularly peaceful tribe and Josephus admits two facts: first, that the man responsible for the gathering "excited them to it"; second, that they *came thither armed*. This, surely, is the most significant feature of the story. An expedition to the ruins on Mount Gerizim, with a purely archaeological or religious purpose, did not call for the carrying of weapons.

In any case, Pilate, hearing that large numbers of men were converging upon the site—*across which lay the main road to Jerusalem*—may well have considered it a necessary precaution to send both horsemen and foot soldiers to the scene. It would appear also that the Samaritans set up a resistance, because Josephus says "it came to an action", during which some were killed, others put to flight, and a great number taken alive. Of the latter, Pilate ordered the ringleaders to be put to death.

Having regard to all the circumstances, and the notoriously restive state of the Palestinian population, I cannot see that Pilate's action went very far beyond that usually taken by a Roman Governor compelled to rely upon a comparatively small military establishment for the maintenance of order. Incipient rebellion had to be crushed immediately it raised its head and Pilate may have mistaken a purely religious movement for something more sinister. Certainly the massing of armed men in the very heart of the Province was something which he could not overlook.

The Samaritan Senate, however, appears to have taken a different view:

> But when the tumult was appeased, the Samaritan senate sent an embassy to Vitellius, a man that had been consul, and who was now president of Syria, and accused Pilate of the murder of those that were killed; for that they did not go to Tirathaba in order to revolt from the Romans, but to escape the violence of Pilate. So Vitellius sent Marcellus, a friend of his, to take care of the affairs of Judea, and ordered Pilate to go to Rome, to answer before the emperor to the accusations of the Jews.

So the historic record of this memorable decade closes, with Pilate and Claudia returning in disgrace to Rome. The Emperor Tiberius died while they were still upon their way and it was to the doubtful mercy of Caligula that Pilate had now to address himself.

CHAPTER XVI

AND AFTER THAT THE DARK

THE only voice which speaks to us from the past with any authority concerning the ultimate fate of Pontius Pilate is that of Eusebius, Bishop of Caesarea, who tells us (*Eccles. Hist.*, 2, 6, 7) that "he was compelled to become his own murderer and the avenger of his own wickedness". This, says the historian, is the account given by those Greeks who have drawn up a list of the Olympiads together with the events of each period.

The rest is darkness, illumined only by the lambent flames of a Dantesque, but undying legend. Yet it may well be doubted whether any human being in history—save, perhaps, Judas Iscariot—has been pursued through the ages with more malignity or with a greater fertility of invention.

The legend, which reached its full flower during the Middle Ages, assumed many strange and even terrifying forms.

It is significant of his deep hold upon the mind and conscience of mankind that the unhappy Procurator should be represented as meeting his death in such widely different circumstances. He dies, successively, for example, under Tiberius, Caligula, Nero, Vespasian and Titus. He is beheaded; killed by an arrow from the bow of the Emperor himself; sewn up in an ox-skin with a viper, a cock, and a monkey[1], as was the custom with parricides; destroys himself in a tower; is swallowed, with the tower, even by the earth itself.

To these portents is added a whole series of nightmares in which the corpse, never at rest, is conveyed from place to place, to the accompaniment of demons and the disturbance of the elements.

At the base of all this fevered imagining is an old Latin legend, the *Mors Pilati*, dating probably from the twelfth century. It is found in its more developed form in a Milan manuscript of the fourteenth century, reproduced by Tischendorf under the title of *Canonical Histories and Apocryphal Legends*. A somewhat similar story appears in the *Golden Legend* (*Legenda Aurea*) by Jacobus de Voragine (1230–98) as the conclusion of the fabulous life of Pilate.

Its language betrays it as hopelessly unhistorical, but since the reader may be interested I give below the late Dr. M. R. James's admirable English summary.

The legend runs thus:

> The Emperor Tiberius, being sorely diseased, heard that there was a wonderful physician in Jerusalem, named Jesus, who healed all sicknesses. He sent an officer of his named Volusianus to Pilate to bid him send the physician to him.

---

[1] cf. the Byzantine chronicler, Georgius Cedrenos, writing about 1070.

Pilate was terrified, knowing that Jesus had been crucified (and begged for fourteen days' delay, *Golden Legend*). On the way back to his inn, Volusianus met a matron called Veronica and asked her about Jesus. She told him the truth, to his great grief, and, to console him added that when our Lord was away teaching she had desired to have a picture of him always by her, and went to carry a linen cloth to a painter for that purpose. Jesus met her, and on hearing what she wished took the cloth from her and imprinted the features of his face upon it. This cloth, she said, will cure your lord: I cannot sell it, but I will go with you to him.

Volusianus and Veronica returned to Rome, and Tiberius, when the likeness was to be brought to him, spread the path with silken cloths. He was instantly healed by looking at the likeness.

Pilate was arrested and brought before the emperor at Rome. Now he was wearing the seamless tunic of Jesus. When he came before the emperor, he, who had been raging against him before, became quite mild. He sent Pilate away and immediately his rage returned. This happened again. Then, either by divine inspiration or on the suggestion of some Christian, he had him stripped of the tunic, sent him back to prison, and shortly after sentenced him to die by the basest of deaths. On hearing this, Pilate killed himself with his own knife. Caesar had a millstone tied to his neck and threw him in the Tiber. The demons gathered in crowds, and storms disturbed the place so that all were in great fear. The corpse was taken out of the river and carried off to Vienne (*via* Gehennae) on the Rhône, with the same result. Thence it was taken to be buried in the territory of Lausanne; but disturbances continued there till the inhabitants dug it up and threw it into a well surrounded by mountains, where diabolical manifestations are still said to occur.

From such fantastic tales—circulated from country to country—arose the identification of Pilate's last resting-place with lonely and haunted regions in Switzerland, Italy and France.

One of the earliest localizations of the legend was at Vienne in France. It is mentioned in the chronicle of Ado, Archbishop of Vienne from 860 to 875. He quotes a passage from Orosius and, confusing Archelaus with Pilate, states that the latter was condemned to perpetual banishment at Vienne, where he ultimately took his own life.

Thus began a tradition which, as the centuries passed, became rooted in the district. One branch of the legend reasserted the old belief that Pilate killed himself in Rome and was cast into the Tiber, whence the body was removed to the Rhône because of the dreadful storms caused by it. Another version has it that Pilate was taken to Vienne for the Emperor's sentence to be carried out and was imprisoned in a tower. There he killed himself and his body was flung into the Rhône. Once again storms arose, the water formed into a whirl-pool, and clouds of demons clustered about the bridge-heads.

Otto of Freising, writing about 1150, states that "he is said to have killed himself with his own sword", but "some say that he was killed in exile at Vienne, a town in Gaul, and afterwards drowned in the Rhône".

In later years tradition associated the place of Pilate's imprisonment with a fourth-century tower which was part of the Roman walls encircling the town. It was known as "Pilate's Tower" and remained until 1769, when it was demolished to facilitate the construction of a quay.

Another curious variant of the Vienne tradition is preserved in *La destruction de Jerusalem et la Mort de Pilate* —a very early printed book of the year 1485. According to this account Pilate was held prisoner at Vienne during such time as a pillar should be made by means of which the Emperor's sentence could be carried out. The story of Pilate's imprisonment in the tower follows and when all traces of the body are lost in the swirling waters of the Rhône we are told that "the column remains in the square of Vienne".

Under the influence of a quite different tradition the Procurator's name came to be associated with a fourth-century pyramid—still to be seen at Vienne—known as "Pilate's Tomb". The suggestion appears to be that, not merely was he pardoned, but became so honoured a citizen that he was accorded burial in a special tomb.

Yet another tradition asserts that Pilate exercised magisterial functions in Vienne and on that account was given a praetorium. The first-century temple of Augustus and Livia, standing to this day, is pointed out as the actual building. On the façade of this temple was formerly a stone ball, known as the "ball of Pilate's sceptre". An inscription to this effect was engraved in the sixteenth century, when the Temple was ravaged in the Religious Wars. The ball disappeared at a later date, perhaps during the French Revolution. The fact that Pilate's name is thus associated, both with the Temple and the

Pyramid, shows that in certain circles in the West—as in Syria and Egypt—the Roman Procurator was viewed in an extremely favourable light. Indeed, in the Coptic Church, Pilate is a Saint, and so is his wife, Claudia.[1]

In Vienne, the two tendencies meet: Pilate is, on the one hand, an honoured citizen, taking part in the public life of the town and, on the other, he is a criminal, to be pursued and killed.

I am indebted to the Abbé Cavard, and to Me. Maurice Faure, both of Vienne, for much valuable information concerning the Vienne legends and for the two interesting reproductions which adorn this chapter.

There is one further object on French soil connected with our subject. This is Mont Pilat, a few miles to the south of Vienne in the Cévennes. Here, in an abyss upon the mountainside, legend affirms that the inhabitants of Vienne were guided by St. Mamert[2] to hide the body. Popular imagination still plays around the mountain. If it stands clear, the weather will be good; if wrapped in clouds, it will be bad. Storms are caused by Pilate.

Johannes Rothe, in his *Passion* of the latter part of the fourteenth century, remarks that when Pilate's body was removed from the Rhône and buried in the ground, heavy stones were piled over it. These soon flew away, however, weird voices were heard and storms began as

---

[1] cf. *The Martyrdom of Pilate*, translated by Dr. Mingana from a rather late Syriac original. The story is similar to that in the *Paradosis Pilati*, existing in a twelfth-century Greek manuscript.

[2] Bishop of Vienne from 450 to 476.

50. VIENNE, ENGRAVING OF MERIAN, 1660

On the left, a wall comes down the hill to a square tower, rising sheer from the river.
This was formerly called Pilate's Tower

51. ROMAN PYRAMID AT VIENNE
(fourth century)
Adorned the middle of the "spina" of a Roman circus. For long considered
to be the tomb of Pontius Pilate

usual. Then the body was removed once more, and taken this time to Lausanne.

The Swiss legends are not dissimilar, and Pilate's name has been associated through the centuries with various haunted mountain tarns.

The localization of the final resting-place of the hapless Roman—first at Lausanne and then on Mount Pilatus, near Lucerne—is closely connected, as in other cases, with natural phenomena. A river is difficult to navigate; a mountain subject to wild storms; an upland pool haunted by medieval enchanters, making use of its remoteness for their own dark ends. Soon popular superstition sought a reason for the storms and in several cases found this reason in the presence of the body and spirit of Pilate, earthbound to the spot for all eternity, seeking vain expiation for his crimes. In such manner did the various Mounts Pilatus in Central Europe take their name.

The Lucerne tradition is very ancient and is met with as early as the thirteenth century in a French MS. (1250) the *Codex parisiensis* in the Bibliothèque nationale. The writer tells how they took Pilate "and threw him into a very deep well, surrounded by great mountains, and still, as many relate, one may notice appearing there very great filths and stinks which the devils make".

At least two writers localized the Pilate-legend near the Rhaetian Alps, namely Gottfried of Viterbo writing about the year 1200 and Conradus de Mure, at the end of the same century. The latter said that the very name of Pilate was dreaded in that district of Switzerland, because, if it were so much as uttered, an earthquake or at least a loud noise would occur.

During the fourteenth and fifteenth centuries the texts multiply—chronicles, poems, Passions—all connecting Pilate with the lake on Frakmont or Mount Pilatus. Pilate becomes a water-demon, sitting on a stool in the lake, with grey hair and beard, attired in magisterial robes, washing his hands. As late as 1666, a traveller is reported to have said that on Good Friday, Pilate was led from the lake to the sea in iron chains.

Italy, too, is full of the legend.

The eighth-century *Cura Sanitatis Tiberii* gives Pilate's place of banishment as a town in Tuscany. A slightly later Latin account, *De Veronilla et de imagine domine in sindone depicta* develops this story. Pilate having killed himself, his body was thrown into the sea, whereupon the fish died. The body was therefore removed and carried by the citizens of Rome to a desert place, "where they knew that no man came".

Now there is in the Apennines, at Norcia, a mountain and a lake which were long considered haunted and the scene of devilry and incantation. Here, throughout the Middle Ages, necromancers and enchanters came to perform their strange rites and to consecrate to the Devil their magic books. Here, too, was a cave of the Sibyl.

The mountain is first connected with Pilate by Fazio degli Uberti, in 1367, who, in his *Dittamondo*, refers to an already established legend:

Fame mentions the mount of Pilate where is a lake which is watched during the summer because he that is learned in Simon Magus goes up there to consecrate his book, whence tempests arise with great fury, as is related by those of the district.

Bernadino Bonavoglia, a preacher at Foligno, embellishes the tale a few years later: "It is said that near Norcia is a certain mountain in which is a lake called Pilate's, because it is the opinion of many that his body was transported thither by devils. . . . To this place come devils' men from near and far."

In the fifteenth century two foreigners visited Norcia and recorded their impressions. One who mentioned Pilate came in 1420; he was the celebrated author of the *Petit Jehan de Saintré*, Antoine de la Salle, soldier, courtier, crusader. He thoroughly explored the caves of the Sibyl and wrote the whole legend in detail in his *Paradis de la Sibylle*. He tells the story of a German tourist who penetrated to the very throne of the Sibyl herself and was lured to stay there, thus giving us an Italian version of the Venusberg.

La Salle did not actually visit Pilate's lake. His interest was chiefly centred in the Sibyl's cave and he was not an ardent climber. He describes it, however, from hearsay, beginning with the current local tale of the death of Pilate and his transportation to the lake at Norcia:

And folk say too that when Pilate saw that there was no remedy for his life, he asked for a boon, which was granted him. Then he requested that, after his death, his body should be put on a chariot, harnessed with two pairs of buffaloes and allowed to go where the buffaloes should chance to take it. And thus they say it was done. But the emperor, who marvelled at this request, wished to know where the chariot would arrive and therefore had it followed until the buffaloes came to the edge of this lake. Then they rushed in with the chariot and Pilate's body as hastily as if they were being pursued. For this reason it is called Pilate's lake.

Pilate is also connected with the Aquila district of the Abruzzi province. It was at Aquila that was "found" in 1580, enclosed in a box of white marble, one of the various copies of the so-called "sentence of condemnation". A legend of Pilate's end clung persistently to the neighbourhood, and as late as 1899 it was still current. Pilate had lived, it seems, in a great palace which he had built for himself on a hill-top. There are certain unexplained ruins to be seen there to this day. When he had unjustly condemned Christ, he repented and retired to his palace near Aquila. The Emperor heard of his crime and sent an army against him; then rats came and gnawed through the foundations of the palace in one night, so that it fell in ruins. Devils then seized Pilate and carried his body one hundred miles away. Finally it was dropped into a river.

Such are a few of the portentous tales which clustered around the name of the Roman Procurator in medieval times. Historically they are worthless; they serve only to emphasize the universal terror and revulsion of feeling occasioned by the recollection of his crime.

It is strange that in all the inspired imagining of Dante's *Inferno* there should be no direct or explicit reference to Pontius Pilate. There is one canto, however, which brings us very near to him:

> for one came now before mine eyes
> Crucified with three stakes upon that floor.
> He, when he saw me, into his beard with sighs
> Blew, and contorted all his limbs as well;
> And Friar Catalano,[1] marking this,
> Said: "He, impaled, on whom thy gaze doth dwell,
> Counselled the Pharisees that it was meet
> That one should suffer for the whole people.
> Naked and cross-wise on the road he is set
> As thou beholdest, and must feel the load
> Of all that pass above him on their feet.
> His father-in-law hath wretched like abode
> Within this fosse, with the others whose consent
> For all the Jews a seed of evil sowed,"
> Then I saw Virgil marvelling as he bent
> Over him outstretch't on the cross, in plight
> So abject, in the eternal banishment.

The man who thus lies, impaled to the ground, is Joseph Caiaphas—the Courtier-Priest with the stately mansion on the South-West Hill, who shared with Pilate those ten uneasy years of rule in Judea, and who ultimately fell with him.

---

[1] One of those in torment, to whom Dante spoke. The quotation is from Laurence Binyon's translation.

CHAPTER XVII

POSTSCRIPT

(Written late one evening in the Palm Court of
the King David Hotel, overlooking the City)

IT was the last night of our stay in Jerusalem. The
moon—nearly full—rose brilliant and clear over the
Mount of Olives, flooding the Garden of Gethsemane
and the walls and roofs of the old city with a cold and
almost ethereal light.

A dance was announced at the "King David" that evening, but I was disinclined to join it, and after dinner I
went into the now darkened Palm Court to gaze once
more upon that incomparable vista of Suleiman's mighty
wall, flanked by the steep declivity of the Bethlehem
road. It is a scene which will always linger in my memory
—the moonlit city, proud and unforgiving as ever, surrounded by her bastions and set securely upon her
immemorial hills.

The distant strains of Strauss's "Blue Danube" waltz
floated through the partially open door into the deserted
chamber. For some moments the familiar tune mingled
with my reverie and then abruptly vanished, for a

242

thought had seized me which had never presented itself quite so vividly before.

I had just completed my work on the Roman Procurator and was trying to recall the scene at Caesarea on that memorable day when Pilate and his wife, Claudia, re-embarked from the great breakwater to commence their melancholy return journey to Rome.

I remembered that the year was A.D. 36.

There was something familiar about the date—something which seemed to be rapping softly, like the signals of an imprisoned miner, upon the walls of memory. Then I recalled suddenly that it was in the summer of that year that the Apostle Paul, now a converted Christian, returned from his solitary communing in the Arabian desert and spent a *whole fortnight* in Jerusalem—a city then not widely different from that which lay before me now.

I fell to pondering two closely related things. Was it conceivable that he could have spent fourteen days in that confined circuit and not once have paid a visit to Joseph's tomb? If he did go there, what were his inmost thoughts and emotions as he stood beside the cave which, according to our modernistic interpretations, contained the loved and lacerated body of his dead Leader?

I am sorry to put it quite so harshly as that, but this is indeed the whole deep fundamental issue with which we shall be concerned in this postscript.

A month earlier, when I left Southampton, the need for such a discussion was not present to my mind. At that time, and at that distance from the scene, it seemed that one could write the essence of Pilate's story, as it were *in vacuo*, without touching more than the fringe of these larger issues.

I was mistaken.

The real Jerusalem was somehow strangely different. For one thing it was surprisingly small. You could put it comfortably into Hyde Park and Kensington Gardens, with some hundreds of acres to spare, and the distance from the reputed tomb to the walls (which I actually checked with a stop-watch) was certainly not more than three minutes. The more I thought of it the clearer it became that the events of that Sunday morning following the Crucifixion—*whatever they may have been*—were too deeply involved in the history to be dismissed in this airy and inconsequent fashion.

Slowly, as I stood there in the moonlight, the whole massive case for the historicity of the women's visit to the grave came back to me, and, more for the sake of my own peace of mind than for the purposes of publication, I sat down there and then and wrote the essence of what follows.

Now there is one thing about this matter which impresses me profoundly. It is not something which has to be "placed" in a favourable light to obtain the effect. You can forget it for years, and yet when you return it still stands stark and uncompromisingly out of the historic picture. I mean the very curious emphasis which all the documents place upon what for our general con-

52. THE "POOL OF HEZEKIAH"

Showing the dome of the Church of the Holy Sepulchre in the background

53. GORDON'S CALVARY
Showing the rocky formation known as the "skull"

venience we will call the post-crucifixion phenomena.

On any normal interpretation of the facts this is directly contrary to logical expectation.

We shall all be agreed, I suppose—looking back now across two thousand years—that in the early part of the first century there appeared in the Province of Judea a spiritual Teacher of quite exceptional range and power; a man who had a gift for saying things, not only in a very fresh and original way, but with a compression of thought almost without parallel. Many professed Jews to-day see in Jesus of Nazareth one of the great prophets of their race and Dr. Sukenik told me that for purely historical and archaeological purposes he was inclined to treat the three Synoptic Gospels as substantially part of the Old Testament.

This great Teacher is suddenly arrested during one of the Feasts—ostensibly on the ground of His subversive teaching about the Temple—and is executed the next morning at the instance of the Jewish Power. His terrified disciples flee, but reassemble later and pledge themselves to carry on the work which He had begun. The rest is history, and the ever-growing dominance of the Christian Church.

Given these historical postulates, what would you expect?

You would expect, surely, to find this nucleus of a new and growing movement going about the world with a message which laid primary emphasis upon the *content of the Teaching*. You would expect to find them saying:

"Here was a great and profoundly good man, an inspired interpreter of the ancient scriptures with a new and vivid gospel for the bewildered sons of men. He was wickedly cut off in the very zenith of His powers. But His message still lives and we will devote our lives to carrying it to the ends of the world."

Actually we find nothing of the kind.

Whether we turn to the Acts of the Apostles or to those far older index fingers, the Epistles of St. Paul, we find the same universal phenomenon. The *primary* interest—the aspect of the matter which clearly gripped everybody —is not so much what Jesus *said* as *who he was*. And at the heart of all this contemporary writing is the confident assertion (as though the fact could not seriously be challenged) that God had raised this man from the dead.

That curious slant and drift of the literary evidence is admitted by all. It comes out in the first sentence of the oldest of the Gospels: "The beginning of the gospel of Jesus Christ, the *Son* of *God*." It is reflected, fifty years later, by the younger Pliny, Governor of Pontus and Bithynia under Trajan, who tells the Emperor in a letter that the Christians

> are accustomed to meet together before dawn and to sing antiphonically a hymn of praise to Christ as God.

Yet, about thirty years after the Crucifixion, when all the initial excitement has died down, and the earliest written records begin to appear, the teaching emerges slowly, as we knew it must. It is like a submerged volcanic island rising by progressive stages from the sea. The higher peaks and the more vivid parables come out first in the Gospel according to St. Mark. Then a vaster plateau emerges in the twin-Gospels of St. Matthew and St. Luke, depending largely upon contemporary notes and recollections of the more arresting sayings. Finally, the picture is completed in the Gospel according to St. John.

It does not seem to me to matter very much whether the reader thinks of the Fourth Gospel as a *poem* or an *historical* narrative. The impressive thing is that its writing was clearly inspired by the historic Jesus, and I venture to say that no other human being in history has come within a thousand miles of inspiring a document like that.

Two broad facts emerge from these considerations.

The first is one upon which, to-day, I feel there will be general agreement, viz. that the historical figure whom we call Jesus of Nazareth was of a *stature commensurate with the dislodgement of events* produced by His history. The Teaching itself, when at length it emerges into full view, sets the seal upon that.

The second, however, is hardly less obvious. I mean the rather startling fact that, *in all human probability*, we should never have heard of this teaching at all had it not been for what we have agreed to designate as the post-crucifixion experiences. This seems to me to stand stark out of the historic picture.

So far as we know Jesus himself committed nothing

to writing. The Lord's Prayer, for example, was uttered by Him in the presence of a small body of comparatively illiterate men, and became by constant iteration engraved upon their memories. The parables of the Sower, the Good Samaritan, the Prodigal Son, and all the other superb examples of His genius, were spoken to little village gatherings and by virtue of their inherent worth sank into the mind. All this, however, was but a ripple upon the surface of a remote backwater of the pagan sea. Who would have troubled to report it had not something far more challenging to the thought and belief of the ancient world been carried by eager and excited men to the confines of the Roman Empire?

The more deeply we reflect upon this situation the clearer it becomes that the post-crucifixion phenomena were the spearhead of the Christian movement in earliest times. It was this which gave it its impetus. It was this which "saved" the Teaching and secured its historical and literary permanence.

We are forced back, therefore, to inquire how it was that the followers of Jesus, and the immense numbers of new converts who rallied to their cause, came to be so undeniably convinced of the survival of Jesus.

Here we have really only three logical alternatives.

The first is the hypothesis of the Twin-Brother. I hesitate to present this to the reader in my own words, lest (without having that intention) I should phrase it unfairly. We have no use for merely verbal quibbles in an issue of this magnitude. Let Dr. Eisler himself put the case. I take the essential passage from page 564 of his book. He is describing the situation immediately after the Crucifixion of Jesus.

> Whoever among his adherents were not dead or captured made off in all directions; the shepherd was beaten, the herd dispersed. Among the women and the few faithful who had remained near to find out, at the dusk of day or at early dawn, what had become of the mortal coil of their erstwhile king, none of course discovered the corpse. What they did see, the one here and the other there was ... the twin-brother of their Master, resembling him in every particular; and that fleeting glance, together with a few stray words caught in passing and doubly significant in that emotion in which they found themselves, was the starting point of the rumours which spread like wildfire that he who had been anointed at Bethainah was really and truly, according to his own prediction, risen from the dead.

From a purely literary standpoint Dr. Eisler has, I think, phrased this passage very skilfully. I doubt if it could be put more cogently. But observe its curious fragility. The supposed meeting of this "twin-brother" has to be limited to a "fleeting glance" and a few stray words "caught in passing", as though one of the disciples encountered a transient cowled figure in the dusk. There is nothing here corresponding to that vivid narrative in St. Luke's Gospel describing the journey to Emmaus or the meeting of the ten in the closed room.

Observe also, that to facilitate the recognition this shadowy figure must needs be a *"twin"*. There is no hint in any extant document that there was more than one birth in the cave at Bethlehem, and it is surely a matter of some significance that neither the *Jew Tryphon* nor even that greater sceptic *Celsus* had apparently heard of the story. If they had, what play would they not have made of it!

Personally I do not envy the man who can silence his historical conscience with this particular hypothesis. That there were "brethren" of Jesus we know, but they are portrayed as hostile, until one joined the crusade and became a revered leader of the church. Ultimately he perished for his devotion to the cause.

The second hypothesis is that usually described as the theory of *hallucination*. It had a considerable vogue about forty years ago, but it is generally recognized to-day as failing to satisfy historical conditions. It is purely subjective in character and presupposes a state of mind in the disciples favourable to the production of a phantom of their dead Leader.

It breaks down completely, however, in the face of the experience of St. Paul, because here is a man who, upon his own confession and the clear teaching of the records, was at first definitely *hostile* to the teaching of the Apostles. He knew perfectly well what the disciples claimed, but was so violently opposed to it that he launched and carried through, on his own initiative, the first great persecution of the Church. Yet it is this man, with his brilliant intellectual equipment, his mastery of dialectic and his deep-rooted initial antipathy to the whole doctrine, who ultimately came over—lock, stock and barrel—to its support. It is almost impossible

to exaggerate the historical significance of this very remarkable fact, which is attested, not only by his close
companion, St. Luke, but by the public correspondence
—marvellously preserved almost in its entirety—of the
man himself.

We are brought, therefore, face to face with the ultimate question: what *will* satisfy all the known conditions
of this very complex historical problem?

And here I want to say something which I feel it is
very desirable to say at this juncture. It concerns the
meaning which we should attach to a word which is
quite unavoidable in this particular connection, but
which is often greatly misused. I mean the word "*super-
normal*". It will avoid some heat and much confusion
of thought if we can agree upon a definition. Personally
I would define it thus:

We can divide the world of experience into two broad
categories:

(*a*) The phenomena which respond to and are completely
explained by our existing knowledge of the Universe.

(*b*) The growing body of phenomena concerning which we
have as yet insufficient data and upon which an ultimate
judgment must of necessity be deferred.

There are reasons for believing that the fully explored
aspects of the universe are relatively infinitesimal compared with the complete (and probably inaccessible)
whole. It is still as true for us to-day as it was for Sir
Isaac Newton that man is to be likened to a child
"playing by the sea-shore—now and again finding a

shell more variegated than the rest while the vast ocean
of truth lies unexplored before him".

The use of the word "super-normal" should not therefore imply anything necessarily transcendental or contrary to ascertained knowledge, but merely recognition
of the obvious fact that many things must and do occur
beyond our present range of logical explication.

Among these, the so-called "Appearances" of Christ
are a classical example. It is illogical to deny them because, if they are totally expelled or eliminated from the
historic field, the history of the first century yields only
an intellectual chaos, a contradiction in terms, a system
without its central and all-controlling sun. Put them
back again and the *logical stresses cease*. The history takes
an assured and comprehensible course.

When, therefore, so profound and convinced a modern-
ist as Professor Kirsopp Lake argues that a purely subjective explanation of the appearances does not satisfy
the historical conditions and supports the theory that
the phenomenon had an objective stimulus—"the manifestation [to use his own words] of a surviving person-
ality"[1]—he is, I think, strictly within the limits of a truly
scientific approach to this great problem.

We do not yet know how so vivid and intense a consciousness of a visible and audible presence was produced
in the minds of the recipients. We only know that the
evidence for it in the Gospels is exceptionally strong.
And behind that great witness is the far earlier and

[1] *The Resurrection of Christ*, Williams and Norgate, London 1912.

54. THE GARDEN TOMB

Believed by many to be the true site of the Burial of Jesus

55. INTERIOR OF THE GARDEN TOMB

The railings with their cruciform embellishment are, of course, modern

authentic voice of Paul, calling to us across the centuries in that ringing passage from his first letter to the Corinthians:

> he appeared to Cephas; then to the twelve; then he appeared to above five hundred brethren at once, of whom the greater part remain until now, but some are fallen asleep; then he appeared to James; then to all the apostles; and last of all, as unto one born out of due time, he appeared to me also.

But the logical pointers of which we have been speaking have one further peculiarity. They set up an equal and even greater sense of stress if we expel from the Gospels that other aspect of the post-crucifixion story, the reported visit of the women to the grave and their failure to fulfil the mission upon which they were bent.

I do not think that the full weight of this fact is appreciated to-day. For consider what is actually involved.

It will be remembered that all the *Synoptic* Gospels—which were written within the lifetime of many present at the fatal Passover—assert quite explicitly that Mary Magdalene, accompanied by some of her friends, went to the grave at dawn. This is confirmed by the surviving fragment of the Gospel of Peter (see page 210). All these documents agree, moreover, upon one vital point, viz. that the women were *prevented* from performing the last rites for which undoubtedly they went. In the words of St. Luke, "they found not" the body of Jesus.

In the Fourth Gospel, however, which frequently gives

us vivid little flashes of light upon historic detail, we read something further. Here again Mary Magdalene is accompanied by her friends (for there is a tell-tale "we" in the passage which follows), but it would seem that after their experience in the garden, Mary herself, who was probably much younger than her companions, *ran on ahead*, and we get a wonderful little vignette of her knocking breathlessly at the door of a certain house in Jerusalem, exclaiming:

> They have taken away the Lord and we know not where they have laid him.

I do not know how the reader will feel, but to me that sentence is an excerpt from real life. It shows no signs of bending to apologetic tendencies. It is the stark, outspoken cry of a woman who set out a few minutes earlier to perform certain rites at the side of One whom she deeply loved—an opportunity which would shortly pass from her for ever.

If you feel like that also, then one thing is certain, viz. that, consciously or otherwise, *an empty tomb* was associated with the Christian story from the very first morning. I am not suggesting here that the women immediately associated their rather disquieting discovery with the survival of Jesus. Clearly they did not. St. John's words imply this and the whole tenor of the *Marcan* account (the earliest of all the records) is to the same effect.

The point which I am now stressing is that, historically, the thought of a vacant grave was no mere "inference" from the appearances, a legend of slow and comparatively late growth. Its association with the story is as old as Christianity itself—as old even as the dawn of that fateful Sunday. It goes right back to the historic core of things and arose out of the peculiar nature of the women's adventure itself.

This is at least something to the good, since it brings home to our minds a fact which is in some danger of being overlooked, viz. that there are *two* aspects of the Resurrection problem which cannot be separated. The cause of truth is not furthered by merely pushing out of sight elements of the story which are inconvenient or even destructive of preconceived theories.

Given that vital postulate, we are free to put the matter to the test.

Let us assume any one of the normal explanations which have been advanced in modern times to account for the failure of the women to locate the body of Jesus. They fall roughly into two categories. There is, for example, Dr. Lake's own suggestion that the women may have mistaken the tomb in the dim light and that the young man whom they encountered within the cave was merely trying to correct their mistake. There is the possibility that Joseph of Arimathea himself, having temporarily used his own tomb for the rather hurried interment, subsequently removed the body to a more suitable and permanent resting-place. Finally, there is the suggestion that the Jewish authorities or the Roman

Power intervened during the week-end and effected a transfer.

All these are perfectly rational contingencies and, if proved, could be accepted by a sincere Christian without serious damage to the basic article of his belief.

It is just here, however, that the logical stresses begin to make themselves felt.

It must be evident to any one who seriously studies this subject that in any of the above-mentioned contingencies, the *real* place of interment must have been perfectly well known to the authorities in Jerusalem and there is no visible reason why, in given circumstances, its identity should not have been revealed.

Let us grant that the disciples, impressed by the far more exciting phenomena of the Appearances, did not lay stress upon the physical vacancy of the grave. This is quite in accord with the picture of their propaganda presented in the earlier chapters of the Acts. Why worry about unessentials when the real proof of survival lay elsewhere?

But it must also be remembered that the High Priest Caiaphas and his father-in-law, Annas—not to mention other highly placed dignitaries of the Jewish hierarchy— had the strongest possible reasons for crushing this heterodox movement from its birth. The Christians were gaining many converts by their confident assertion of the Resurrection of Jesus. The authorities could not hope to convert the leaders, but they had it in their power, not only to check the spread of the movement, but to deliver to it a peculiarly fatal blow. It was not even necessary to produce the body. A cold official statement, declaring the known place of interment, with an assurance that it was intact, would have carried conclusive weight to the vast mass of Jewry. A fierce controversy would then almost certainly have started, in which one side asserted the Resurrection and the other side quoted the official disproof.

Now the arresting thing is that, while the echoes of many such controversies have been preserved, *this is not among them*. You can search the apocryphal literature through and through and find almost everything except that for which we are now looking.

We hear a great deal, for example, about the anger of the priests towards Joseph of Arimathea, in respect of his unauthorized approach to Pilate for permission to bury the body. We get snatches of a heated debate over the accusation that Jesus was "born of fornication". We are even told that Pilate himself searched for the body and found it in a neighbouring well. There is also the curious suggestion that *Judas Iscariot* "took the body of the Fatherless" and concealed it beneath a watercourse.

But when we go right back to the earliest document outside the Gospels—the very primitive Gospel of Peter (c. A.D. 150)—we find deeply embedded therein, as in the case of our own St. Matthew, the *Story of the Guard*.

Now the peculiarity of this story is that whether we regard it as fact or fiction it yields the same unvarying result. If fact, the vacancy of Joseph's tomb was ascertained by the authorities themselves. If legend, it could only have been used by the Christians as a means of rebutting the very damaging assertion that they had stolen the body. This deliberate lie that the disciples had abducted the corpse of their great leader is one of the clearest and most certain echoes of those far-off times.

When we remember the urgency of the Jewish need for some indisputable refutation of the disciples' claim, the intellectual vigour and resource of the unconverted Saul, the facility with which the Christian guns could have been spiked by an official disclosure of the true facts about the interment, it is surely deeply significant that what seems to have been the hottest corner of that salient should be upon ground which tacitly admitted the *inability*, even of the bitterest opponent, to bring forward the one certain, final and unanswerable argument.

We reach, therefore, two broad conclusions. I will try to formulate them with some care:

First. The "appearances" of Jesus, as described in the Gospels —seen in their historical and consequential aspects—seem to indicate the *manifestation of psycho-physical phenomena of a very unusual kind*, and must therefore be placed provisionally in our first category, i.e. of events concerning which we have as yet insufficient scientific or experimental data.

Second. The suggestion that the Christian campaign in Jerusalem, prior to the first Persecution, was (or could have been) conducted consciously in the physical presence of the remains of Jesus, *lying by the mutual consent of both sides within three minutes' walk of the Gennath Gate*, raises logical stresses[1] of a very grave order—a sort of deformation of history which suggests that here also is some concealed factor of vital import.

Historically, we can carry the investigation no further. We can only await that fuller light which time, and our growing knowledge of this strange universe will assuredly shed upon it.

Many years ago, however, when the bleak monism of Haeckel lay like a blight upon the otherwise fair prospect of philosophy, I came to the conclusion that a Universe so depicted was *too uninteresting to be true* and I staked my intellectual peace upon the belief that when light should at last fall upon these deep questions it would come from the scientific rather than the theological side.

The ferment of recent years has justified that conclusion to the hilt.

Of all the stony and fruitless questions which encumbered the field of New Testament criticism in the days of my youth none was more fiercely contested than the statement (reported, of course, by all the Synoptic writers) that Jesus of Nazareth predicted the destruction of Jerusalem.

Immense efforts were put forth by the textual critics to show that these Gospels were written after the vital

---

[1] This sense of logical stress is greatly increased when we recall that John Mark and Luke the physician were at various times the companions of St. Paul. The story which they ultimately told in their Gospels must have been deeply coloured by the apostle's personal belief, yet both writers assert most emphatically the vacancy of Joseph's tomb.

date (A.D. 70) and that the very vivid and precise language attributed to Jesus was coloured by the knowledge of the event. Slowly the critical issue was fought out until Harnack proved (I think quite conclusively) that St. Mark's Gospel at least, and probably all the Synoptics, were in existence for some years prior to the catastrophe. Even the *Acts of the Apostles*, as the critic demonstrates at great length, contains no hint either of the fall of Jerusalem or of the death of St. Paul.

About nine years ago my interest in this subject was re-aroused by the publication of Mr. J. W. Dunne's extraordinarily interesting and suggestive book, *An Experiment with Time*, in which he advances very strong scientific reasons for believing that both in our dreams and in our waking experiences there are integrated elements of *past* and *future* events. For the documentation of this very singular "effect" the reader must turn to Mr. Dunne's book, but it set me thinking along new lines. Here was evidence of a concrete and experimental kind which tended to show that, not only could one dream vividly of a future event (see discussion of Claudia's dream, page 195) but that with suitable safeguards one could pick up *stray traces in the waking mind* of books one was *going* to read and of events which one had *yet* to experience.

I transferred in imagination the whole theory to the field of theology. I said in effect: here is a clear case of a document published, say, not later than A.D. 65, containing a perfectly clear and definite prediction of the

destruction of the Temple in A.D. 70. Would history—
especially modern history—afford any parallel? The most
likely parallel which came into my mind was the Great
Fire of London in 1666. This had the advantage of
coming within the era of printed books, and publishers
have a commendable habit of inserting dates upon their
title-pages. Here, therefore, was an opportunity to test
Dunne's effect upon a large historical scale.

To my surprise I found quite indisputable traces.

As Mr. Walter Bell, the historian of the Fire, has
pointed out, it is impossible to read through the literature
of the Commonwealth and the early years of the Restoration without being aware of "a vein of gloomy prog-
nostication of impending catastrophe. . . . The idea lay
like a nightmare over the religious feeling of the time.
In conventicle and Quakers' meeting-house the pulpits
resounded with the utterances of those who railed in no
measured terms against the monster city . . . proclaiming
with the fervour of fanaticism that the measure of her
iniquities was full and that the day of extinction was at
hand". (*The Great Fire of London*, page 18.)

It is significant that in at least five printed prophecies
the calamity is clearly foretold as coming by *fire*. Thus
Walter Gostello, in a treatise dated 1658, speaks of fire
making "ashes of the city". "London, London [he de-
claims], sinful as Sodom and Gomorrah, the decree is
gone out. Repent or burn." Daniel Baker, in a tract
dated 1659, has a similar prophecy in which he speaks
of "a fire, a consuming fire . . . which will scorch with

burning heat all hypocrites . . . fire and smoke shall increase . . . and great wailing shall be on every hand in all her streets". Humphrey Smith, a famous Quaker, who died in Winchester Gaol four years before the Fire, prints a remarkably accurate pre-vision of the actual devastation in a pamphlet published in 1660, entitled *The Vision I saw concerning London:*

> All the tall buildings fell. As I passed through her streets I beheld her state to be very miserable. . . . And the fire continued, for although all the lofty parts were brought down yet there was much old stuffe and parts of broken down desolate walls which the fire continued burning against. And the vision thereof remained in me as a thing that was showed me of the Lord.

A private contemporary letter (also quoted by Mr. Bell), describing the catastrophe, refers to the numerous printed predictions of the Fire and Pepys has, of course, told us that when news of the burning reached Prince Rupert, then on the high seas, he remarked that now "Shipton's prophecy was out".

These things are significant.

They show that in a four-dimensional world—the only world of which we have any knowledge—many confident conclusions based upon the older physics, and especially upon the *pre-Minkowski concepts of the nature of Time*, are invalid. 1658–1659–1660! Save for the practice of the Restoration typographers in putting dates upon their work, how many reams of valuable paper might not have been used by textual critics, seeking to prove that these indisputably historic documents were written after the event?[1]

Consider now another aspect of this unexpected drift in modern thought.

When I was a young student, in the early '90's, one of the most fixed of the contemporary ideas about the universe was expressed in the phrase: "The Plurality of Worlds". The idea that the stellar bodies are inhabited by highly intelligent forms of life goes back to the Greeks, but it received a tremendous impetus from Galileo's discovery of the telescope. As far back as 1686 Fontenelle wrote a book which was published in Paris and went through many editions, in which he maintained that the moon and the planets were inhabited. The idea was taken up by Alexander Maxwell in 1820, by Whewell in 1823, and developed during the Victorian era by Chalmers, Sir David Brewster, Proctor and others. It was the mode to think of the universe as teeming with

---

[1] It would be out of place to discuss here the many curious consequences of applying the newer concepts of Time to the field of moral philosophy. Consider, for example, the case of a man who commits what is called a "perfect murder". A subtle and scheming brain conceals or destroys every visible trace and providing the murderer carries his secret to the grave it may well seem that he has escaped its penalties. Who shall reconstruct a scene which no human eye beheld, when even the physical relics of the victim have long since dissolved in decay? But stay. In Minkowski's world present and past *co-exist* and it will avail the delinquent nothing if some Avenging Angel, disdaining the cumbrous machinery of our earthly Courts, should take him, as it were, by the ear and confront him by *himself* in the act of committing the murder. Does not some awful possibility like that lie at the root of the agonized cry of the Psalmist that a Merciful and Omnipotent Deity should *blot out* his iniquities? In the Courts of God a man's past may be his sole accuser. "What need have we of further witnesses?"

bursting life, and I can remember my father, a voracious student of such works, arguing gravely that even the sun might have its own special adaptations.

The century closed—and then came a bombshell.

In the year 1904, Alfred Russell Wallace, the co-discoverer with Darwin of the principle of Natural Selection, published a book called *Man's Place in the Universe*. Wallace was a highly competent biologist and in nearly three hundred pages of close reasoning he showed that protoplasm—from which all life springs—has a very narrow margin of tolerance, both in respect of atmospheric content and temperature, and he reached two very remarkable conclusions:

(1) That no other planet in the solar system than our earth is inhabited or habitable.

(2) That the probabilities are almost as great against any other sun possessing inhabited planets.

The book was received in most quarters with incredulity and scorn. The whole idea was contrary to that "settled picture of the Universe" of which religious modernism so frequently speaks. Then came 1914 and the fog of war enveloped for some years the work of our scientists.

Meanwhile certain things had begun to emerge. It was realized that life as we know it could only arise in stellar systems which have *planets* and it was found that the birth of a planet is a highly exceptional occurrence. Not fewer than one-third of the stars accessible to our telescopes are *binary* stars, which, for dynamical reasons, cannot have planets at all, and calculations show that the chances against the formation of a system of planets in the minority of stars which are not binaries are of the order of one hundred millions to one! Indeed, so high are the odds that Sir Arthur Eddington, one of the foremost of our mathematical physicists, has written this remarkable paragraph:

> I do not think that the whole purpose of the Creation has been staked on the one planet where we live; and in the long run we cannot deem ourselves the only race that has been or will be gifted with the mystery of consciousness. But I feel inclined to claim that *at the present time* [Eddington's own italics] our race is supreme; and not one of the profusion of stars in their myriad clusters looks down on scenes comparable to those which are passing beneath the rays of the sun. (*The Nature of the Physical World*, page 178.)

Do you remember the superb imagery of Milton who, in *Paradise Lost*, speaks of Satan rising defiantly from the pains and penalties of hell and descrying far off in the empyreal heaven:

> This pendent world, in bigness as a star
> Of smallest magnitude, close by the moon.
> Thither, full fraught with mischievous revenge,
> Accursed, and in a cursed hour, he hies.

When did we first hear this strange story of a cosmic experiment *gone wrong*, demanding some unique and drastic treatment? Was it not in the writing of an aged fisherman, looking back from the seclusion of the lovely isle of Patmos upon a supremely memorable and probably unique experience: "God so loved the world that he gave his only-begotten son, that the world through him might not perish but have eternal life."

What a stumbling block those two words, "only *begotten*" have been to the faith of many, who recognize in the remainder of the saying a profound truth! Yet have we really taken the measure of the possibilities?

I suppose no one to-day will have the presumption (or the conceit) to imagine that man is the highest form of intelligence in the universe. Neither can he logically maintain that this bloodstained planet is a credit to any rational being, least of all to us. What if the Miltonic conception should happen to be *true*—true in the deeper and more actual sense that some Supreme Servant of that awful and impenetrable Mystery we call God, undertook of His own volition to see what could be made of life on this planet—to set a new and undying standard which should shed a light like a beacon across the stormy seas of time.

Is not that the *essence* of the Christian doctrine of the Incarnation? And possibly the sole reason why those curiously candid documents, the four Gospels, so steadily refuse to yield to us anything but that strangely logical Figure, the Christ of Faith.

I have only one other word to add. It will be very brief and the reader may, if he wishes, regard it merely as a parable.

For many years there has stood in an honoured place

in my library a book written in 1902 by Henry Latham, Master of Trinity Hall, Cambridge, entitled *The Risen Master*. Latham was famous as the author of *Pastor Pastorum* and a great deal of his book is a continuation of the same theme. But there are three chapters at the very beginning of the work which have a sort of timeless freshness, as though they stood out, not from some theological treatise which must dim with age, but from some queer text-book of the remote future.

The attention of Latham was attracted by an obscure and now very rare monograph, written by the Rev. Arthur Beard (a wrangler of St. John's College, Cambridge, in 1855 and later Chaplain of King's) entitled *The Parable of the Grave Clothes*. This caused him to make a very close study of the original Greek of the passage in St. John's Gospel which describes the visit of the disciples Peter and John to the tomb of Christ. It is an extraordinarily vivid, close and scholarly study, written with a curious detachment of mind, as though the writer were looking objectively over the shoulders of the two men into the tomb.

It is quite impossible to do justice to Mr. Latham's brilliant textual analysis in a brief summary and the interested reader is referred to the book itself. But the conclusion he reaches—expressed by him very logically and convincingly—is that the writer of St. John's Gospel was trying to convey to us something peculiar and unexpected in the disposition of the grave-clothes, something which gave him the impression, not that they had been hastily thrown aside, but that the body had, as it were, been *withdrawn* from them, as the Time-Traveller in Mr. H. G. Wells's brilliant romance "withdrew" from the sensory presence of his friends. The verisimilitude of Mr. Latham's analysis, stressing the peculiar meaning of the Greek words employed, is remarkable and owes nothing to any conscious desire to establish a particular theory.

These are clearly speculations beyond our present competence even to discuss, but it seems to me an extraordinary, and perhaps a significant, thing that it should be possible to extract from the *Gospels themselves*, without force and with a meticulous regard for the original meaning of the Greek, an interpretation of the greatest of all mysteries, which shows so close an affinity to the more recent concepts of relativist physics.

What if, centuries hence, in the fuller light of a more enduring philosophy, Latham should prove to have been *right*, as Alfred Russell Wallace was right about the Plurality of Worlds, and John Mark, the friend and contemporary of Paul, was right about the destruction of Jerusalem?

NOTES ON THE LITERATURE

THE standard works on the history and archaeology of Palestine are too well known to need special mention here. The writer has already expressed his deep indebtedness to Sir George Adam Smith, whose classic study (*Jerusalem*, 2 vols., Hodder and Stoughton, London, 1908) embodies most of the assured results of recent exploration. The same writer's *Historical Geography of the Holy Land* is also invaluable to the student. A comparatively little-known work on Ancient Caesarea (*Cäsarea am Meer*, by Dr. Leo Haefeli, Munster, 1923) may be consulted with advantage. A modern study of the Roman Procurator (*The Letters of Pontius Pilate to his friend Seneca*, by W. P. Crozier, Jonathan Cape, London, 1928) while, of course, purely imaginative, contains many acute observations and is worth perusal.

The writings dealing with the Pilate legends are numerous, but not all of the same value. In the following notes, a distinction should be made between "primary" and "secondary" sources, i.e. those dating from early times which served in the formation of the Pilate legend, and modern critical works, containing a section devoted to one or more aspects of the legendary tales.

The majority of the Early Fathers refer to Pilate, and their works may most conveniently be used in Migne's monumental collection, the *Patrologiae Cursus Completus*; particular mention may be made of Eusebius, Orosius, John Malalas and Georgius Cedrenos. Tertullian should be read in the Loeb edition. The first apocryphal references to Pilate are in the so-called *Gospel of Peter*, and the earliest definitely legendary material is the *Acta Pilati*, dating from some time before 376. Already in c. 150, however, Justin Martyr had spoken of the existence of some such papers as the *Acta*. There is a reference to Pilate in the *Doctrine of Simon Cephas in Rome*, published in Cureton's *Ancient Syriac Documents*, 1864, from a fifth-century Syriac text in the British Museum.

The Eastern legend, favourable to Pilate, especially in its Coptic form, is to be found in E. Revillout's *Les Apocryphes coptes* [in *Patrologia orientalis*, T. ix. ii, 1923], in the *Anaphora Pilati* [in *Sinaitic Studies*, No. 5, 1896], and it is also advisable to see W. E. Crum's *Some further Meletian documents* [in Journal of Egyptian archaeology, 1927]. Mingana's *Woodbrooke Studies* edition [Cambridge, 1928] of *The Martyrdom of Pilate* should be considered with some circumspection, but it is nevertheless important.

The Western legends of Pilate's end may be said to be founded on the theme of the *Mors Pilati* [published by Tischendorff in his *Evangelica apocrypha*, 1853], existing in various forms, such as the *De vita et origine perfidi ac miserrimi perditoris Pilati* [Cologne ? 1485]. This is similar to certain texts contained in Mone's *Anzeiger f. Kunde der teutschen Vorzeit* for 1835 and 1838, where also may be found some of the Germanic legends of Pilate. Others are in H. F. Massmann's *Kaiser Chronik, Bibl. d. geschichte deutsche National-Literatur*, Leipsig, 1854, Abth. 1, Bd. 4, Th. III, pp. 569-621. L. Weiland's *Niederdeutsche Pilatuslegende* [in *Zeitschrift f. Deutsches Alterthum*, 17, Berlin 1874] and Creizenach's *Legenden und Sagen von Pilatus* [in H. Paul's Beiträge. . . . Vol. 1, Halle, 1874] are valuable. So is Goedeke's Historical Poetry [*Grundriss z. Geschichte der Deutschen Dichtung*, 1, pp. 60-2, Dresden, 1884], especially for the legends of Pilate's birth. Much helpful matter is to be had in two excellent studies of Pilate, namely G. A. Mueller's *Pontius Pilatus, der funfte Prokurator von Judäa und Richter Jesu von Nazareth*, Stuttgart, 1888, and H. Peter's *Pontius Pilatus, der Römische Landfleger in Judäa* [in *Neue Jahrbücher f. d. Klassische altertum, Gesch. u. deutsche Literatur* Leipsig, 1907].

Some medieval works about Pilate are of a general character, such as the *Cura Sanitatis Tiberii*, the *Vindicatio Salvatoris* [including an Anglo-Saxon variant, in the Bodleian Library], St. Gregory of Tours' history, Otto of Freising's *Chronicle* [c. 1150] and Jacobus de Voragine's *Golden Legend* [thirteenth century].

The location of Pilate's death in different spots is shown in various works. The principal ones centred upon Vienne in France are the history of St. Ado, Bishop of Vienne in the ninth century, passages in variants of the *Mors Pilati*, the anonymous early printed book *La destruction de Jerusalem et la Mort de Pilate*, [1485], Johannes Rothe's *Passion* [published by A. Heinrich in 1906, from a Dresden MS. of the fifteenth century], Aymar du Rivail's *de Allobrogibus libri novem* [1550], Jean du Bois's *Viennae antiquitates* [1605] and Jean Le Lièvre's *Histoire de l'antiquité . . . de la Cité de Vienne. . . .* [1623].

References may be found in several of the above-mentioned books to the Swiss Pilate legend as well, and there exists in addition a very good and thorough modern study by P.-X. Weber, entitled *Der Pilatus und seine Geschichte . . . Lucerne*, 1913. Two MSS. are also important, first the *Codex Parisiensis*, French, thirteenth century, and secondly Gottfried of Viterbo's *Speculum Regum* [early thirteenth century], MS. at Vienna. The *Dictionnaire historique et biographique de la Suisse* [1930-4] and the *Enciclopedia italiane* [just completed] contain detailed and admirable articles on the Pilate legend.

Finally, the manifestations of the legend in Italy are noted, or studied in the following, as well as in references in some of the early works such as the *Cura Sanitatis Tiberii: De Veronilla et de imagine domini in sindone depicta*, Fazio degli Uberti's *Dittamondo* [1367], a sermon of Bernadino Bonavoglia [in a fifteenth-century MS., quoted by A. Graf], Antoine de la Salle's *Le Paradis de la Reine Sibylle* [edition used, Paris, 1930], and two modern studies of great value, namely A. Graf's *Miti, leggende e superstizione del medio evo*, II, Torino, 1893, and G. Pansa's *La leggenda abruzzese di Ponzio Pilato* [in *Rivista abruzzese di scienze, lettere ed arti*, xx, fasc. III, 1905].

An excellent modern translation of the more important apocryphal works in which reference is made to the Roman Procurator will be found in Dr. M. R. James's *The Apocryphal New Testament*, Clarendon Press, Oxford, 1924. Attention is also directed to Dr. Thackeray's well-known English version of the *Jewish War* (Loeb Classical Library, Heinemann, London), which includes an appendix upon the Slavonic additions. The corresponding translation of the *Antiquities* is still in progress.

INDEX

273

INDEX